Welcome to

START SMART, FINI$H RICH!

The first edition of *Baker's Dirty Dozen* was published as *Principles for Financial Independence* in December 2020. It was ranked the #1 book by *"Financial Education For Everybody,"* a partner of Amazon, in their Financial Literature Category, and was also recognized by GoBankingRates.com as one of the *"10 Financial Books That Will Change Your Life (and Finances)."*

Now, we are excited to bring you our second edition of *Baker's Dirty Dozen Principles: Start Smart, Finish Rich!* This updated edition features:

- ✓ Fresh, up-to-date financial insights
- ✓ Inspiring new stories and contributions from readers and colleagues
- ✓ Practical tools to help you build financial independence

We can't wait for you to read it—and we believe you'll find it even more valuable than the first edition.

"I thought this would be another dull finance book I'd never finish—but I was wrong! *Baker's Dirty Dozen* is smart, clear, and surprisingly fun. Joe and Lindsey Baker have made personal finance approachable—even for people who hate thinking about it. I just wish I'd had this book when I was younger."

HARRY THOMASON, Hollywood director and producer (*Designing Women, Hearts Afire*) and author of *Brother Dog Southern Tales* and *Hollywood Adventures*

"I'm 55. I needed to read Joe Baker's book when I was 25. Thankfully, I found a similar book back then by Frances Leonard called *Time Is Money*. Both books show examples of the power of compounding interest to drive home the point that saving and investing money at an early age is critical. Our kids are now in their mid-20s, and *Baker's Dirty Dozen* can help them prepare for a better financial future. As KATV's 7-On-Your-Side reporter for 20 years, I saw how easy it was for scam artists to trick Arkansans with get-rich-quick schemes. Joe's book can help people protect their money not only from traps but also from other forms of financial ruin. Plus, you will learn some proven investment paths. 'The path to financial freedom, while not always easy, is not a mystery either.' Peppered with real-life stories from fellow Arkansans, this book seeks to increase financial literacy in a state that needs it."

JASON PEDERSON, former KATV 7-On-Your-Side reporter and author of *Somebody's Knocking*

"If every student about to graduate could just understand these 13 principles the Bakers teach in this book, they could avoid so many financial mistakes and build wealth. If you're serious about getting ahead, this is your financial cheat code."

SARAH CATHERINE GUTIERREZ, CFP®, CRPS®, founder of Aptus Financial and author of *But First, Save 10*

"Reading this book will change your life. Joe Baker and Lindsey Baker take decades of financial wisdom and deliver it in a way that's both accessible and actionable. The Bakers created a masterful page-turner that is brimming with practical financial advice that readers can apply in their daily lives. A must-read for anyone serious about financial independence!"

DR. BETH ANNE RANKIN BAKER, coauthor of *The Economics of Freedom: In Defense of Capitalism*, vice president of Good Work Partnership, LLC, and Rankin Consulting, Inc.

"This book—and the practical advice it offers—has guided me from buying a used car in graduate school to purchasing my first home and setting up investment portfolios. It's been the most valuable resource for helping me feel confident about managing my money, instead of letting it manage me."

DR. KARLEE CARNEY, assistant professor of pharmacy practice at Belmont University, Nashville, TN

"This is one of my favorite books! I buy them for all of the young adults in my life. I really should buy them by the case—it's that good!

STACY AUSTIN, realtor at RE/MAX DFW Associates, Flower Mound, Texas

"After taking Joe Baker's personal finance class and reading *Baker's Dirty Dozen*, my wife and I were inspired to tackle our $214,594 in student loans, and we paid it all off in just 17 months. Today, we're completely debt-free. Our full story is featured in this book."

DR. LEVI ELLISON, Ellison Pharmacy

"*Baker's Dirty Dozen* is the best self-help book I have read in my 80 years. It is very organized and well-written but not pedantic. Information can be useful to young or old, 'haves or have-nots' or those in between—in other words, almost everybody. I wish I'd had it when I was much younger; then, among other things, I wouldn't have made the 'time-share mistake' that I have lived to regret. One example among the many nice features is a section called 'Resources for Budgeting' in which the authors list apps for internet sources that may be beneficial for more detailed information, forms, etc. Best of all, I really enjoyed the quips and funny anecdotes that were used to illustrate some of the messages or experiences."

RACHEL SHIREMAN, Amazon reviewer

"I enjoyed reading *Baker's Dirty Dozen*, not only for the entertaining stories that he tells in his book but also for the way he lays out financial decisions clearly and concisely. He adds his own advice throughout (notice the Baker's Choice headings), but his opinion is not overpowering. I felt like I was able to read the book, come to an understanding of a topic, and then make my own decision. The most helpful chapter for me was the chapter about retirement planning. It helped me understand not only the value of investing early, but also what to invest in wisely. I will be applying the principles from this book in my own life and look forward to a life of financial independence!"

RACHEL SENN, Amazon reviewer

BAKER'S DIRTY DOZEN SECOND EDITION PRINCIPLES

START SMART, FINI$H RICH!

The Smart, Simple Way to Build Wealth While You're Young

JOE BAKER, MBA   LINDSEY JORDAN BAKER, MAT

Paperback ISBN (KDP): 979-8-9930533-3-2
Paperback ISBN (LSI): 979-8-9930533-5-6
Case Laminate ISBN (KDP): 979-8-9930533-4-9
Case Laminate ISBN (LSI): 979-8-9930533-6-3
eBook ISBN: 979-8-9930533-2-5

BUS027030   BUSINESS & ECONOMICS / Finance / Wealth Management
EDU013000   EDUCATION / Finance
SEL027000   SELF-HELP / Personal Growth / Success

Publishing coordinated by Authors Who Lead
Cover design and typesetting by Kaitlin Barwick
Edited by Valene Wood

themoneycheatcode.com

With Deep Gratitude to Every Contributor

Your personal stories have breathed life into the pages of this book. You've helped transform financial concepts into real, relatable experiences, and in doing so, you've made this book not only more engaging but also more impactful. Thank you for being an essential part of its success.

Thank you to all my former personal finance students from the past 26 years who inspired me to begin this journey.

CONTENTS

Foreword by
DR. MARY ANN CAMPBELL, CFP®

a.k.a. Dr. MAC, MoneyMagic.com

MY NAME IS MARY ANN, and I'm a SALE-aholic.

A bargain is something I don't need at a price I can't resist. If it's a 1/2 of 1/2 sale, I struggle to maintain dignity.

I've tamed my cravings through a lifelong commitment to financial education. Having taught personal finance at the college level for 38 years, been a fee-only certified financial planner practitioner for 35 years, and earned my PhD with a personal finance focus at Iowa State University, I am a committed money educator.

Joe Baker is the kind of personal finance educator from which I wish our three boys had been given the opportunity to take a class. In fact, our granddaughter, Whitney Campbell, did take his personal finance class during her final year at the UAMS College of Pharmacy. Whitney would light up when she talked about Joe Baker's class and what she was learning. "He actually showed us his Dillard's credit card statements and what he and his wife spent their money on. I'm not sure his wife knows how much he shares. I look forward to his class and am learning things I'm going to use!"

And that is what you'll find in this book—now and in the future—to improve your financial life. You'll put it down refreshed and not feel at all beaten up for past mistakes. Although raised on a farm and spending more time on the same farm since his recent retirement, he serves no bull in this, his first book. He is direct, to the point, and serves up pertinent information derived from years of experience teaching personal finance to third-year pharmacy students and observations of the quirky things we all do with our money. To be more relevant to multiple generations, Joe Baker's book is co-written with one of his two beautiful daughters, Lindsey Baker.

Read this book and reap a sense of security, financial well-being, a comfortable retirement, peace of mind with your significant other, and smiles—many chuckles and smiles as you travel Joe Baker and Lindsey Baker's life experiences managing their money. The lessons are so profound and poignant that you may want to share them with those you love and care about. So dig in and enjoy *Baker's Dirty Dozen Principles*.

DR. MARY ANN CAMPBELL, CFP®
Edu-tainer and President of Money Magic, Inc.

Foreword by
TIMOTHY ULBRICH, PharmD

YourFinancialPharmacist.com

In 2012, I had a humble realization that despite making about $500,000 of income since graduating from pharmacy school, I had a net worth of negative $225,000.

A net worth of negative $225,000 put a spotlight on my spending habits and forced me to face the reality that I wasn't making much progress on paying down my debt, let alone growing my assets.

Having a net worth of negative $225,000 was the motivation I needed to change my financial situation. I would never look back from this point in time.

Besides the mountain of student loan debt I had accrued (about $200,000), there was one main obstacle standing in my way to financial freedom: a sub-par education in personal finance. Yes, I had lots of obstacles in my way (lots of debt, poor spending habits, and lack of savings, to name a few), but underneath all of these was a poor foundation in my knowledge and application of sound financial principles.

As I read through *Baker's Dirty Dozen Principles* for the first time, I thought to myself, "Where was this book when I was in pharmacy school?!" This book would have transformed my understanding of personal finance, and I'm confident it will do that for you as well.

Baker's Dirty Dozen Principles provides a simple and engaging way to learn personal finance principles that will set you free. This resource is overflowing with Joe Baker's wisdom, his life experiences, and his more than two decades of teachings.

As you begin reading this book, take time to reflect upon the following question: What does it mean to you to achieve financial independence?

My personal experience teaching thousands of pharmacists about this topic suggests that the answer to this question is different for everyone. Taking the time to reflect upon and answer this question is foundational to the rest of your financial plan. It will be your guiding path and motivation when things get tough. It will also define the milestones that deserve pause and celebration along the way. And, last but not least, it will be the place from which you will inspire and teach others.

As you dive into this book, I encourage you to first read through in its entirety and then keep it handy for a specific Baker's Dirty Dozen Tip (or two) that is most timely and relevant to your current situation. I have realized that the learning never ends when it comes to personal finance. I plan to keep this book nearby and hope you will do the same.

As you turn the page and get started, know that you are beginning a journey that will forever change your life. After reading *Baker's Dirty Dozen Principles*, I'm confident you will never look at your money in the same way.

Onward to financial freedom!

DR. TIMOTHY R. ULBRICH, PharmD
Co-Founder and CEO of Your Financial Pharmacist

INTRODUCTION

JOE'S STORY

I didn't grow up with a financial plan; I grew up with an outhouse.

Our small family farm was just outside of Emerson, Arkansas, population 393. On the farm itself, there were five of us, plus a few cows, chickens, dogs, and horses. We didn't have indoor plumbing until I was nine years old. But somehow, it never crossed my mind that we were poor, after all, our outhouse had *two* holes instead of one! Not that I remember ever sharing it. I do, however, remember the Sears catalog.

The first time I sensed we might not have much was when I asked about the Magnolia Country Club. My Granny Bradley looked over and said, "Oh honey, you have to have a bathtub full of money to go there." That line still rings in my head.

I graduated in the top 10 of my class at Emerson High School—not the top 10%, but the literal top 10. There were 28 of us. But even with good grades, college wasn't something my family talked about. My dad worked in construction, and as soon as I could carry a bale of hay, I was working too, for 6¢ a bale. That was the *generous* rate. When I worked for my dad, I didn't get paid at all. "I'm feeding you, aren't I?" he'd say. I started making sure to charge him "overtime" every time I stuck my legs under his table.

Still, I knew early on I wanted a different path. I was determined not to spend my life on construction sites or in hay fields. So I enrolled at Southern Arkansas University, just 15 miles up the road. If it had been any farther, I'm

1

not sure I would have gone. Student loans were off the table. My dad thought college was a waste of time, and borrowing money to do it? Forget it.

College was a fresh start. I took on two or three jobs at any given time and got involved in campus life. I didn't graduate in the top ten (or top 10%) of my college class, but I was elected Student Body President my senior year. I majored in business, not because it was my passion (history was), but because I wanted to be able to support myself.

I won't bore you with every job I held before getting married at age 30. Let's just say life gets *really* interesting once kids enter the picture.

At age 29, I had a bed (no headboard), a TV, a VCR (you can Google it), and some credit card and car loan debt. When I met my wife, a high school math teacher, she saw two things: (1) no furniture conflicts and (2) potential. As they said in *O Brother, Where Art Thou?*, I was "bona fide." She helped whip me into financial shape.

Most of my adult life was spent working at Pharmacists Mutual, a company that provides insurance and financial services. Later, I went back to school and earned an MBA. The most valuable thing I got from that degree? Understanding a financial calculator, time value of money, and opportunity cost. That knowledge, along with the financial wisdom I absorbed through "math teacher osmosis," helped us create a strong foundation.

Here's a look at our financial timeline as a roadmap I now share with others:

- **30**: Got married with more debt than savings (yep, we started in the red).
- **31**: Paid off everything except the mortgage.
- **31–50**: Stuck to our plan—saving steadily for retirement, living below our means, and avoiding new debt.
- **50**: Paid off the house and became completely debt-free.
- **52**: Our savings hit a milestone we never imagined when we started out.
- **59**: That number grew even more—not from luck, but from years of patience, discipline, and compound interest doing its thing.

It took decades to build momentum, but once things clicked, the growth really took off. That's the power of staying consistent, avoiding debt, letting compound interest work its magic, and trusting the long game.

Fast forward and I have now spent over 26 years teaching personal finance as an adjunct instructor, retired from a successful career, and traveled the country as a speaker, promoting financial literacy to both academic and corporate audiences. I share this not to boast, but to reflect. There's plenty I would do differently if I had the chance to go back. With the clarity I have now, particularly in my 70s, I can see just how much more intentional and effective my financial decisions could have been before my 30s. Experience sharpens vision.

That's why I'm writing this book—to leave a legacy that outlives me.

On many occasions, my former personal finance students would often come back to me years later and say, "I still remember that story you told about . . . " And that's the key: stories. Stories are how people connect with ideas that might otherwise feel dry or intimidating. That's why you'll find this book filled with them—funny, real, and often hard-earned. Many are from contributors who've been in the trenches of financial decisions and want to pass along what they've learned.

This book doesn't contain magic secrets. In fact, most of the advice here is shockingly simple. But financial literacy is still shockingly rare. This book will give you a roadmap to financial independence, one that works regardless of your income level, background, or profession.

It's designed to bridge the experience of the Baby Boomer generation with the passion, purpose, and energy of younger generations. Together, we can chart a path toward financial independence in a way that's clear, practical, and available to anyone willing to walk it.

LINDSEY'S STORY

In college, life was simple. I didn't have a car, bills, or much real responsibility. I had a modest savings account from high school jobs, but most of my needs were already covered. The "real world" still felt far away, like something I could ease into at my own pace.

At the time, I was more interested in figuring out the philosophy of life than the mechanics of money. One of my required courses was Personal Finance, but I sat in the back of the room, half-listening as the professor went on about amortization and risk tolerance. It all felt too technical, and I didn't see how it connected with my financial life. I passed the class with a B but left with very little I could actually use.

It wasn't until years later that I realized how important that class should have been. Like most students, I had gone through high school and college without ever learning how to create a budget, manage debt, understand interest, or build long-term savings. These weren't just missing pieces; they were the foundation.

And it's not just an individual issue. We're graduating young adults into a complex economy armed with little more than a diploma and a vague sense that money matters, but no clear understanding of how to manage it. The consequences of this are far-reaching. Financial illiteracy doesn't just affect one person's budget; it ripples out through families, communities, and generations.

A financially unprepared population is more vulnerable to debt traps, predatory lending, financial anxiety, and long-term insecurity. It makes people more dependent, less empowered, and often stuck in cycles they don't know how to break. It holds back progress not only on a personal level, but on a societal one.

Like many young adults, I brushed it off until life forced me to pay attention. Once I did, it all started to make sense.

Now, with over a decade of experience teaching middle and high school students, I've learned how to take complicated financial concepts and make them relevant, real, and usable. That's exactly what we hope to do with this book: bridge the gap between what's taught in a classroom and what's needed in life. When we equip people with financial knowledge, we don't just change bank accounts—we change futures.

Baker's Dozen

"A group of 13; a dozen plus one: from the former practice among bakers and other tradespeople of giving 13 items to the dozen as a safeguard against penalties for short weights and measures."[1]

1. Dictionary.com, s.v. "baker's dozen," https://www.dictionary.com/browse/baker-s-dozen.

Baker's Dirty Dozen

PRINCIPLE #1

Find a Path That Will Fulfill You

If you're hoping this book will unlock the secret to becoming a millionaire by 25 while doing yoga on a beach in Bali . . . well, good luck. This isn't that kind of book. But if you want practical, no-fluff advice to help you get ahead financially, then you're in the right spot.

According to Wikipedia (yes, we still use it, and yes, it's still free), *self-actualization* means becoming everything you're capable of becoming.[1] That idea comes from psychologist Abraham Maslow and his famous Hierarchy of Needs.[2]

Maslow basically said: First, get your basics covered such as food, water, a roof over your head, and a working toilet. Then comes stuff like friendships, confidence, and, finally, living with purpose. Later in life, Maslow added one more top tier—*transcendence*, which means living for something beyond yourself. (And no, I didn't learn this at Woodstock. I was only 14 at the time.)

Here's what I've learned after decades of trial and error, starting barefoot in rural Arkansas and working my way up: You don't need to have it all figured out. But you do need a plan.

This book isn't about chasing money for money's sake. It's about giving you a financial foundation that lets you build the kind of life you actually want, without wasting decades getting there.

That starts with finding your path.

---

1. *Wikipedia*, s.v. "self-actualization," https://en.wikipedia.org/wiki/Self-actualization.
2. Saul McLeod, "Maslow's Hierarchy of Needs," *Simply Psychology*, August 3, 2025, https://www.simplypsychology.org/maslow.html.

Notice I didn't say, *"Find a job that fulfills you."* That's a bonus, not a requirement. For some people, work is a calling. For others, it's a paycheck that funds the stuff that really matters—family, passion projects, volunteering, travel, art, whatever.

The point is, you get to define success. And in today's world, it's more possible than ever to align how you make money with who you actually are.

HARRY THOMASON: How I Ended Up in Film

In 1966, I was coaching and teaching in Little Rock at a job I loved with people I admired. But after six years, that close-knit staff began to move on, and I had a decision to make. I'd always loved photography and art, and I figured if I was ever going to chase that dream, now was the time.

So, I jumped into advertising without any experience. I started drawing imaginary TV commercials after track practice, sketching out storyboards frame by frame. My fellow coaches chimed in with opinions, usually while laughing.

Then I read a news story: Frank Whitbeck, president of a national insurance agency, was planning to run for governor. His ad agency was named in the article, and I figured, "Why not me?" I sketched campaign spot ideas that night and, without an appointment, walked into their downtown office.

The receptionist was kind; Jim Brandon was . . . skeptical. I heard him say, "Why are you wasting my time with someone who isn't even an amateur?" But, shockingly, he agreed to see me.

I pitched him, "I'll produce the spots at my own expense, and if you don't like them, you don't pay." He raised an eyebrow and said, "You've got one day with the candidate—Saturday morning. I'm crazy for doing this."

I left both thrilled and terrified. I had no camera, no crew, and no clue. Back at school, I told the other coaches. They laughed, then said, "How can we help?" We borrowed equipment from Ray-Chris Productions (after they stopped laughing too) and trained ourselves late into the night.

We were football coaches turned filmmakers.

We found a horse ranch for the shoot, bought matching green T-shirts and ball caps (because why not look the part?), and met at 7 a.m. sharp. When the candidate stepped out of his black sedan and asked, "Are you from Dallas?" I realized he had no idea he was talking to a bunch of coaches and jocks.

Somehow, it all worked. The footage looked great, and Brandon admitted, "The footage looks very good." Our ads aired, the candidate won the primary, and although he lost the general election, we got a congratulatory note and a foot in the door.

That's how I ended up in film. Just the beginning of one wild, wonderful ride.[3]

Author's note: Harry Thomason went on to a successful career in Hollywood, producing, directing, and writing hit shows such as *Designing Women*, *Evening Shade*, and *Hearts Afire*.

FINDING YOUR OWN PATH

According to the Bureau of Labor Statistics, Americans between the ages of 18 and 37 hold an average of nine different jobs.[4] In the past, we may have viewed this as a sign of failure. But today, it's a sign of exploration. These years are filled with trying things on for size: different jobs, different cities, different dreams. You're figuring out what fits, what doesn't, and what actually matters to *you*.

You're not behind. You're not lost. You're learning.

And that learning isn't just about finding the right career, but it's also about understanding how to build a stable, flexible life that gives you choices. Because the truth is, no matter what path you take, money is going to walk alongside you. It can either trip you up or help you move forward.

So . . . what kind of path are you on?

This chapter is here to help you reflect on that question. And the rest of this book? It's designed to give you the financial tools, mindset, and confidence to walk your path, whatever it looks like, with purpose, clarity, and a whole lot more freedom.

---

3. Harry Thomason, "How I Ended Up in Film," in *Borther Dog: Southern Tales and Hollywood Adventures* (Parkhust Brothers, 2019).
4. U.S. Bureau of Labor Statistics, *The Economics Daily*, "People Born Between 1980 and 1984 Held an Average of 9.0 Jobs from Ages 18 through 36," June 26, 2024, https://www.bls.gov/opub/ted/2024/people-born-between -1980-and-1984-held-an-average-of-9-0-jobs-from-ages-18-through-36.htm.

A New Kind of Workforce

Since the early 2000s, people have built entire careers in ways that didn't exist when I was starting out. YouTubers. Freelancers. TikTok creators. Podcasters. Coders. Consultants. Folks running businesses from their phones in coffee shops.

We've invented new terms like *side hustle*, *vlogging*, and *creator economy*. We've embraced texting shorthand, emoji communication, and Slack culture. And while some traditional jobs are disappearing, new ones are popping up all the time.

Technology has opened doors. The challenge now is walking through the right one.

Fulfillment Comes First

Before you chase a job or title you think you "should" want, pause and ask: What actually brings me energy?

Here are a few examples of what that might look like:

- Maybe you want to travel the world and see how others live.
- Maybe you want to write a bestselling novel.
- Maybe you want to make your home HGTV-worthy.
- Maybe you want to open a brewery, launch a business, or teach high school students.
- Maybe you want to give back to the community that raised you.

Whatever it is, fulfillment doesn't come from luck. It comes from *intentionality*.

Job vs. Career vs. Calling vs. Gig

Type	What It Means	Good If You . . .
Job	A way to pay the bills	Need short-term income
Career	A field you grow in over time	Want stability and progression
Gig	Short-term or flexible work	Want freedom or extra income
Calling	Work that feels deeply meaningful	Want to align purpose with profession

You don't have to pick just one. Many people cycle through all four at different stages in life.

Career Path

The 8-hour workday became a cultural norm during the Industrial Revolution, thanks in part to social reformer Robert Owen, who coined the phrase: "Eight hours labor, eight hours recreation, eight hours rest."[5] That was revolutionary at the time. Fast forward to today, and the 40-hour workweek often feels like a minimum rather than a standard. Many professionals now work 50 or more hours just to keep up in our hypercompetitive economy.

Because a job takes up a third of your life and plays a major role in your financial and emotional well-being, it's worth asking: Does your job contribute to your fulfillment?

Signs You Hate Your Job—and What to Do About It

Hopefully, you're one of the lucky ones who enjoys your work. But if you're not, don't panic, because you're far from being alone. Start by taking inventory of your skills, interests, and values. What are you good at? What do you enjoy doing? These questions can help you start aligning your talents with new opportunities.

How do you know if it's time for a change? Here are some red flags:

- ✗ You dread Monday mornings and feel it physically—tension, headaches, stress.
- ✗ You no longer care about your performance or the organization's mission.
- ✗ You've lost interest in growing within your role.
- ✗ You take more sick or mental health days, or wish for reasons to skip work.
- ✗ Your job feels like a burden, not a calling.

And sometimes, the signs are a little more . . . dramatic.

A friend of mine, Ron Lester, once worked as a junior accountant. One day, while operating a massive shredding machine, his mind wandered . . . right as his tie got caught in the blades. Thankfully, a coworker unplugged the machine in time. Ron took it as a sign that it was time to "cut ties" with corporate life.

---

5. Marguerite Ward, "A brief history of the 8-hour workday, which changed how Americans work," CNBC, May 3, 2017, https://www.cnbc.com/2017/05/03/how-the-8-hour-workday-changed-how-americans-work.html.

Before You Quit, Try This

Not every career rut requires a resignation letter. Sometimes, what you really need is rest, reflection, or a shift in routine. Before making a major move, ask yourself: Am I burned out, or do I just need a break?

Here are some things you can try first:

- ○ **Talk to your boss.** Could your role be reshaped? Flexible schedules, remote options, or shifting responsibilities might bring new energy to your work.
- ○ **Change your environment.** Get more sunlight, take regular breaks, and step outside for fresh air. Even small changes can help you feel more grounded.
- ○ **Find joy outside of work.** Volunteer, start a hobby, join a rec league, or take an online class. The Yale course "The Science of Well-Being" is free on Coursera and is a powerful reset.[6]
- ○ **Take a mental health day.** Your brain needs rest just like your body. Apps like "Waking Up" by Sam Harris can help you practice mindfulness and recalibrate.[7]
- ○ **Make space for connection.** My wife and I have spent 40+ years playing cards with the same group of friends every weekend. Laughter, community, and a good margarita can do wonders for the soul.

When You're Ready for a Career Change

If you've tried to reset and you still feel stuck, it may be time for a change. Just do it strategically.

A few key guidelines:

- **Don't leave your current job until you have another one.** It might feel good to storm out in a blaze of glory (ask my daughter who quit by lunchtime on her first day), but it's better to have your next step lined up.
- **Do your research.** Talk to people in the field you're interested in. Read job descriptions. Watch videos. Shadow someone if you can.

6. Enroll for free at https://www.coursera.org/learn/the-science-of-well-being.
7. Try a free trial at https://www.wakingup.com.

- **Expect challenges.** No job is perfect. Sometimes it's not about escaping difficulty but finding the right kind of challenge for your skills and goals.
- **Consider finding a counselor.** The National Career Development Association (NCDA) can connect you with certified professionals who help people navigate these transitions.[8] Or check out Careershifters.org, whose motto says it all: *"Life's too short to be unhappy at work."*
- **Read the New York Times bestseller, *What Color Is Your Parachute?*** by Richard N. Bolles—a trusted guide for job hunters and career changers. Be sure to check for the latest edition, as it's updated regularly.

Before You Leap, Ask These Five Questions

1. Do I hate this career or just this job?
2. Am I burned out, or simply under-challenged?
3. What do I want *more of* in my next role?
4. Can I afford to make a career change right now?
5. Who can I talk to who's already made a move like this?

---

8. National Career Development Association, "Looking for Career Help?", https://www.ncda.org/aws/NCDA/pt /sp/career_help.

CREATE YOUR LIFE VISION PLAN

At the beginning of each semester, I ask my personal finance students two key questions:

1. If money were not an issue, what would your life look like?
2. If your doctor told you that you had 10–15 years left, how would you live?

We talk about how the answers to those questions should help shape their financial plan.

When my wife and I were engaged, we went through six weeks of boot camp, er, I mean, premarital counseling. There were several components to the course. One was a written psychological exam that I had to take *twice*. The first time I took it, the report came back that said, "No one is that perfect." I kid you not. The second part of that process was creating a written "vision plan"—mapping out our career, financial, and personal goals. At the time, it felt like busywork. Even after all of this homework, we still got married! But 15 years later, we stumbled upon that old document, and to our amazement, nearly every goal had come to fruition, even having two children. *signal eerie music*

There's something powerful about putting your plans on paper.

I now have my students complete a life vision plan for their final semester project. Sure there's a little grumbling, but the long-term feedback is overwhelmingly positive.

If you want help getting started, check out "The Ultimate Guide to Creating a Life Vision" by Craig Ballantyne.[9]

So, what does *your* ideal life look like? And what kind of career will help support it?

---

9. Craig Ballantyne, "The Ultimate Guide to Creating a Life Vision," *Early To Rise*, July 18, 2023, https://www.earlytorise.com/ultimate-guide-creating-a-life-vision/.

JASON REECE: From Salsa Dinners to Seven Figures

This is the story all about how my financial life got flipped-turned upside down. It's the story of how I went from living off free chips and salsa, calculating beer prices by the ounce at Mexican restaurants, to becoming a millionaire by age 33 . . . and eventually learning that money alone doesn't buy a full life.

I grew up in South Carolina with parents who were *serious* about saving. Like, rinse-and-reuse-Ziploc-bags serious. In our house, money wasn't just tight—it was sacred. A resource to be guarded. Spent with caution. Sometimes spent never.

Between bickering with my brother, stealing candy from the drugstore (hey, I was a kid), and trying to make the most out of an overly "budget-friendly" childhood, I started obsessing over careers that came with big paychecks. Of course, I hadn't exactly figured myself out yet, so that eliminated options like "police officer," which was sadly scrapped early on.

After scraping by with a glorious 2.7 GPA in high school (yes, we're talking barely-above-the-curve brilliance), I was rejected by my dream school, the University of South Carolina, and ended up at a smaller college instead. But don't worry, I had a plan. High school was practice; college was game time.

Freshman year, I turned it on—3.9 GPA, Freshman Scholarly Achievement award, and an invite into the school's Freshman Honor Society. Boom. I transferred to USC, but this time *with* an academic scholarship, and double-majored in Management and Marketing. Somewhere in between working part-time jobs and poorly trading stocks from my dorm room, I caught the finance bug and made it my mission to build wealth, save smart, and invest wisely.

Fast forward nine years. I was climbing the corporate ladder at a $400 billion company, working hard, investing consistently, and still living below my means. By age 33, I hit a personal milestone: liquid millionaire status. Not bad for a kid who used to count quarters for Taco Bell.

But here's the thing. Growing up in a frugal household taught me to *save*, but it didn't teach me to *spend*. I became hyperfocused on building wealth—sometimes at the cost of actually living. I found myself hoarding money like it was an apocalypse bunker, skipping out on experiences my younger self would've dreamt of.

Eventually, I realized I wanted to do something my parents didn't: enjoy it. Travel. Eat the sushi. Take the trip. Upgrade the seat once in a while.

As I got older, I started questioning everything I'd learned from my boomer parents. I also tried to understand the millennial mindset as the generation that seemed to value freedom, fulfillment, and quality of life in a way I hadn't before. What came out of it? A sort of "Millennio-Boomer" philosophy. A hybrid mindset that believes:

- Save your money . . . but don't forget to spend some on living.
- Work hard and take pride in what you do . . . but don't work yourself into the ground.
- Be a responsible, contributing member of society . . . but choose a life that actually brings you joy.

At the end of the day, the point isn't just to have money. It's to build a life you love.

"Stop and smell the roses,
but don't get caught up in the thorn patch."

Mac Davis and Joey Baker

PRINCIPLE #2

Make Sure Your Significant Other Has the Same Financial Goals as You

You're dating someone amazing. You hike together, binge Netflix, maybe even throw in some disc golf. The chemistry is real. The laughs come easy. The vibes are great. So naturally, the big question is coming . . .

"Are you in debt, and what are your spending habits like?"

Not what you were expecting? Maybe not. But if you plan to build a life together, it's one of the most important questions you'll ever ask. I know, I know. You are marrying for love, not money, but whoever thought up that line must have been a Hallmark movie script writer. This is not a knock on the Hallmark Channel, because I do watch most of their Christmas movies each year, but they are unfortunately unrealistic.

WHY IT MATTERS

It might sound unromantic, but financial compatibility is one of the top predictors of relationship success. According to a 2023 study by Ramsey Solutions, money fights are the second leading cause of divorce, just behind infidelity.[1] And it makes sense: money isn't just about dollars; it's about values, stress, risk tolerance, and life goals.

---

1. Ramsey Solutions, "Money, Marriage, and Communication," *Ramsey*, September 27, 2021, https://www .ramseysolutions.com/relationships/money-marriage-communication-research.

Whether you're planning a future together or already in one, you have to get financially aligned or you'll end up pulling in different directions. That tension builds over time, and it doesn't go away by itself.

HOW TO TALK ABOUT MONEY WITHOUT KILLING THE MOOD

Financial conversations *should* start early—before joint accounts, co-signed leases, or wedding venues. These talks help you understand how your partner approaches money, and whether your habits and goals line up. Discussing these matters on the first date, however, might lower your chances of having a second, so make sure your timing is right!

Try easing into it with simple, natural questions like:

- Do you see yourself owning a home someday?
- What's your approach to credit cards?
- Are you more of a spender or a saver?
- How do you feel about budgeting or long-term planning?
- Is one of us open to staying home if we have kids?

It's not about judgment—it's about clarity. You're not just marrying a person. You're partnering with their financial habits, too.

ASPEN HUSEMAN: The Financial Inquisition

(Or How I Knew He Was the One . . . with a Credit Score Question)

About seven months into dating my fiancé, Hayden, he hit me with what I now lovingly call The Financial Inquisition: "What's your credit score? Do you have any debt? What's your budget? Are you investing?"

I half expected him to pull out a spreadsheet and a laser pointer.

I was caught completely off guard and a little stressed. I did my best to answer, though my responses weren't exactly award-winning. No one had really taught me about personal finance. Growing up, our entire money education could be summed up with: "Don't spend what you don't have." Solid advice, sure, but not much help when someone's asking about your long-term investment strategy over dinner.

Fast forward a year, and I found myself enrolled in Mr. Baker's personal finance class at UAMS—the same one Hayden had taken the year before. Suddenly, everything started to make sense. I laughed at a skit Mr. Baker performed about the financial talks couples should have before getting married. Then I hit Principle #2 in his book: "Make sure you and your significant other have the same financial goals." Lightbulb moment.

Turns out, Hayden had come straight from that class, fully armed with all the "right" questions.

Thankfully, he waited until month seven to unleash them.

Now we're engaged.

So I guess I passed the test—or at least showed enough potential for a follow-up interview.

TOOLS TO BUILD FINANCIAL COMPATIBILITY

If you're thinking long term, don't just wing it. Use the tools available to build alignment and avoid surprises:

- **Be honest about all debt:** Student loans, credit cards, auto loans—lay it all out. The burden will be shared either way. Transparency builds trust.

- **Make your goals visible:** Write down your short-term and long-term financial goals individually, then compare and discuss them.
- **Premarital counseling:** Many counseling programs offer modules on finances. These sessions help you talk openly about money and avoid resentment later.

> "Money might not buy love—but love without
> financial honesty is on borrowed time."

And if you want a little entertainment with your lesson, watch *The Heartbreak Kid* (warning: R-rated). Ben Stiller's character thinks he's marrying the perfect woman . . . until the honeymoon. It's a comedy, but there's truth in the chaos. A little premarital honesty would've saved him a lot of stress and his sanity.

Finances are just one part of compatibility. If you want a more adventurous test, try a two-day canoe trip down a river. You'll learn a lot about teamwork, communication, and patience in a short amount of time . . . if your relationship survives.

This comes from personal experience, of course.

Snow skiing trips work too, especially if one of you doesn't know how to ski. If your relationship survives icy falls, lost gloves, and the stress of ski rental lines, you're probably meant to be together.

FINANCIAL COMPATIBILITY CHECKLIST (BEFORE YOU SAY "I DO")

- ○ Are we both open about our debt?
- ○ Do we agree on budgeting styles?
- ○ How do we feel about joint vs. separate accounts?
- ○ Are we saving for retirement?
- ○ How do we handle financial stress?
- ○ What are our long-term goals (kids, house, career shifts)?
- ○ Would either of us want to pause our career for caregiving or parenting?

○ Do we have shared values when it comes to giving, saving, and spending?

It's easy to get swept up in the romance and ignore the "business" side of a relationship. But marriages aren't just built on love. They're built on trust, communication, and a shared vision, especially when it comes to money.

Take the time to align your financial goals early. It could save you years of stress and help you build a future where both of you are rowing in the same direction.

KRISTEN MINTON J.D., LL.M., CPA:
Love, Liens, and Letters from Virginia
(a.k.a. Why You Should Do a Background Check Before Saying "I Do")

The second my husband and I bought a house in Arkansas, the Commonwealth of Virginia came knocking—digitally, of course. They tried to slap a lien on our brand-new home because my husband, years earlier, had moved away from Virginia and never informed them that his property was no longer subject to their taxes.

Instead of handling it like a responsible adult, he chose a different path: ignoring the hundreds (yes, hundreds) of letters they sent over the course of a decade. He just filed them away . . . mentally . . . in the trash.

Enter me: newly married and instantly co-owner of a house with a side of tax drama.

And yes, I'm completely serious when I say—before you get married, run a lien search, court records check, and pull a full credit report on your significant other.

P.S. I still would've married him. But a little heads-up would've been nice.

TOO LATE, I'M ALREADY MARRIED.
NOW WHAT?

So you're already married. Now what? The most important thing you can do is make sure you and your spouse are on the same financial page, especially when it comes to long-term goals.

According to a study by Ramsey Solutions on money, marriage, and communication:[2]

- Money is the #1 issue married couples argue about.
- 86% of couples who got married in the last five years started out in debt.
- The higher the couple's debt burden, the more likely they are to argue.
- Couples in healthy marriages are much more likely to talk about money, dreams, and long-term goals.

So what's the #1 tool for avoiding money fights? Communication.

Remember the line from the classic 1967 movie *Cool Hand Luke*? (Okay, you probably don't, but stick with me.) The prison warden says to Paul Newman's character: *"What we've got here is a failure to communicate."*

It's funny, until it's your marriage.

For some reason, money is one of the most taboo topics in relationships. But the only way to grow financially as a couple is to talk openly and often about your situation. That means:

- Talking about debt
- Setting shared goals
- Making spending decisions together
- Checking in regularly, even when things are going well

If talking one-on-one feels awkward, consider attending a financial workshop or even doing a budgeting class together. Sometimes a shared activity can open the door to better conversations.

---

2. Ramsey Solutions, "Money, Marriage, and Communication," *Ramsey*, September 27, 2021, https://www .ramseysolutions.com/relationships/money-marriage-communication-research.

On my second date with my future wife, I knew she was the one. Not because of chemistry or common interests but because of a paper towel. One of her guests tossed away a paper towel roll that still had one glued-on sheet clinging to the core. My now-wife *dug it out of the trash*, unglued the last sheet, and set it aside to use later. At that moment, I knew that we were a match, and I fell in financial love! The other kinds of love followed.

LIVING TOGETHER?
TALK ABOUT THIS FIRST.

According to the U.S. Census Bureau, the number of unmarried couples living together tripled between 1996 and 2018, from 6 million to over 19 million. These couples tend to be older, more diverse, and more financially independent than in decades past.[3]

But financial compatibility still matters. Whether you're legally married or not, living together means shared responsibilities, and shared risks.

Start with a conversation:

- Who pays what?
- Is it a 50/50 split or based on income?
- Who manages the bills?
- What happens with existing debt?

Expense Sharing Example

Lucy N. Sky makes $60,000/year as a teacher. Her partner, Buford Murford, earns $25,000/year managing a convenience store. Their monthly household expenses total $1,000.

- **Flat Split:** Each pays $500
- **Proportional Split:** Lucy pays 70% ($700), Buford pays 30% ($300)

---

3. Benjamin Gurrentz, "*Unmarried Partners More Diverse Than 20 Years Ago*," U.S. Census Bureau, Current Population Survey, Annual Social and Economic Supplement, 1996–2018, September 23, 2019, accessed August 28, 2025, https://www.census.gov/library/stories/2019/09/unmarried-partners-more-diverse-than-20-years-ago.html.

Neither answer is wrong—it just depends on what feels fair and sustainable. The important thing is that you agree together.

> **BAKER'S TIP:** Set up a joint checking account *just for shared expenses* (like rent, utilities, and groceries), while keeping personal accounts for everything else. Then decide whether you'll contribute equal amounts or by income percentage.

THE DEBT, THE LOAN, AND THE LESSON

Be wary of co-signing loans or making major purchases together unless you're legally protected. That dream car, house, or shared credit card could turn into a nightmare if your partner ghosts you, or worse, ghosts with your money.

Let me tell you about a friend of a friend (we'll call him Nada Clue). Nada was engaged and used a student loan refund check to buy a car—for his fiancée. She suggested putting the car in her name "for convenience." Two months later, she broke off the engagement and kept the car. Ouch.

Shared debt is serious. Treat it that way.

WHEN KIDS ENTER THE PICTURE

Whether you're married or cohabitating, once kids are involved, every financial decision affects more than just the two of you.

Questions to consider:

- Will one partner stay home? For how long?
- What are your childcare plans and budget?
- What values do you want to model around money?

Having children often forces couples to rethink time, income, and priorities. Talk about it early and often.

EDWARD P. BUERKLE, RPH:
You Had Me at "I Hate Paying Interest"

When it comes to marriage, thinking similarly is far more important than thinking identically. You don't need a clone or a "mini-me," but you do need someone who sees life through a similar lens, especially on the big stuff. In my experience, the five most common stress points in a marriage (in no particular order, and likely to shift over time) are:

1. Sex
2. Money
3. Kids—whether to have them, how many, and how to raise them
4. Time—how much is spent at work vs. together
5. Religion

When my future wife and I were getting serious, we had the money talk. She launched into how she handles finances—budgeting, saving, planning for the future. A few minutes in, I raised my hand and said, "Just stop. Please. Stop."

She looked like she was about to be really mad.

Then I smiled and said, "You had me at . . . 'I hate to pay interest.'"

That was the moment I knew we'd be just fine.

PRINCIPLE #3

Invest in Appreciable Items, Minimize Depreciable Items

In 2018, NFL quarterback Kirk Cousins signed a fully guaranteed three-year, $84 million contract with the Minnesota Vikings, briefly becoming the highest-paid player in NFL history. Despite his massive earnings, Cousins maintained a remarkably modest lifestyle by driving a dented van passed down from his grandmother for years and eventually buying a used Mercedes at a steep discount. Even after signing a $180 million contract with the Atlanta Falcons, he continued living in his in-laws' basement in Atlanta.[1]

"You don't know how long you're going to play," Cousins said. *"You've got to save every dollar even though you're making a good salary."*[2]

It's not just humility—it's strategy.

But here's the catch: not every high earner has a strategy. In fact, many don't. That's why so many professional athletes, despite jaw-dropping salaries, end up struggling financially just a few years after retiring.

1. Nidhi, "$180 Million QB Kirk Cousins Reveals He is Still Living in His In-Law's Basement in Atlanta," *The Sports Rush,* April 07, 2024, https://thesportsrush.com/nfl-news-180-million-qb-kirk-cousins-reveals-he-is-still-living-in-his-in-laws-basement-in-atlanta/.
2. Kevin Clark, "Why the Redskins Players Are So Frugal," *Wall Street Journal,* January 5, 2016, https://www.wsj.com/articles/why-the-redskins-players-are-so-frugal-1452014607.

HIGH INCOME, LOW NET WORTH: THE ATHLETE TRAP

Professional athletes earn massive salaries:

- NBA median salary: $6.7 million[3]
- NFL median salary: $860,000[4]

And yet . . .

- 60% of NBA players go broke within five years of retirement.[5]
- 78% of NFL players experience financial distress within just two years.[6]

Why? Because they invest in lifestyle instead of assets.

INVEST IN APPRECIABLE ITEMS, MINIMIZE DEPRECIABLE ITEMS

Let's start with a simple truth: It's not about what you earn; it's about what you grow.

You could earn millions of dollars and still go broke. Or you could earn a modest salary and retire wealthy. The difference? It lies in your ability to invest in *appreciable* items while minimizing your spending on *depreciable* ones.

3. Ryan Phillips, "What's the Average NBA Salary for 2024–25 Season?" *Sports Illustrated,* September 18, 2024, https://www.si.com/nba/whats-average-nba-salary-for-2024-25-season.

4. Paul Rudder, "What is the average NFL player salary," *AS USA,* September 3, 2025, https://en.as.com/nfl/what -is-the-average-nfl-player-salary-n-3/.

5. *ESPN 30 for 30 – Broke,* Sports Conflict Institute, accessed September 3, 2025, https://sportsconflict.org /resource/espn-30-for-30-broke/.

6. Pablo S. Torre, "How (and Why) Athletes Go Broke," *Sports Illustrated,* March 23, 2009, https://vault.si.com /vault/2009/03/23/how-and-why-athletes-go-broke.

Appreciable vs. Depreciable: What's the Difference?

- ✓ **Appreciable items** are things that increase in value over time or help you build long-term wealth. Think: investments, real estate, education, or starting a business.
- ✗ **Depreciable items** are things that lose value the moment you buy them. Cars, clothes, gadgets, furniture—they may bring short-term satisfaction, but they rarely help build your financial future.

The secret to building wealth? Spend less on depreciating stuff and more on assets that grow.

These are some examples of appreciable and depreciable items:

Item	Type	Why It Matters
Roth IRA contribution	Appreciable	Grows over time with compound interest
Brand-new car	Depreciable	Loses 20–30% of value the moment you drive off
College degree	Appreciable*	Boosts lifetime earnings (*if ROI makes sense)
Latest smartphone	Depreciable	Becomes outdated within a year or two
Rental property	Appreciable	Can generate income and increase in value

What This Means for You

You don't have to be a millionaire to fall into the same trap. The $600/month truck payment. The $5,000 couch financed at 12% interest. The closet full of clothes worn once. It adds up.

But so does smart investing.

> "If Future You won't benefit from it, maybe
> Present You shouldn't buy it."

Start making intentional choices:

- ✓ Choose index funds over impulse buys.
- ✓ Pay off debt instead of upgrading tech.
- ✓ Prioritize savings before splurging on status symbols.

You don't have to live like a monk. But every dollar you spend is a vote for the kind of future you want. Are you voting for comfort today, or freedom tomorrow?

WHEN ENOUGH IS NEVER ENOUGH: UNDERSTANDING LIFESTYLE CREEP

A concept that these people didn't let hinder them in their wealth accumulation is coined in a term called "lifestyle creep." Sounds like I'm making it up, doesn't it? Google it! No, lifestyle creep doesn't mean you're living a creepy lifestyle. But it *is* sneaky.

Lifestyle creep is what happens when your spending gradually increases as your income rises. What once felt like a luxury becomes your new baseline, your new "normal." That $5 latte that used to be a treat? Now it's your daily morning ritual. Upgrading your phone every two years used to feel excessive, but now it feels like a necessity. This shift isn't usually planned. It just . . . happens.

The core of lifestyle creep is something psychologists call *hedonic adaptation*.[7] It's the tendency for humans to quickly return to a relatively stable level of happiness despite major positive or negative changes. In other words, we get used to nice things fast, and then they stop feeling special.

At its worst, lifestyle creep tricks you into thinking you're better off financially because you're earning more, when in reality, your spending has grown so much that you're no closer to financial independence than you were before. In fact, you might be worse off if your new habits include more debt.

Modern Examples of Lifestyle Creep

Today's world makes it easier than ever to fall into the trap, especially with how much "everyday luxury" is marketed to us. Some common signs of lifestyle creep include:

- ✘ Subscribing to five or more streaming platforms (but still saying "there's nothing to watch")
- ✘ Ordering food delivery several times a week instead of cooking
- ✘ Booking more premium travel or upgrading flights as the default
- ✘ Using Buy Now, Pay Later services to afford tech, clothing, or vacations

---

7. "Hedonic Adaptation," *ScienceDirect*, in *Advances in Motivation Science*, 2018, accessed September 3, 2025, https://www.sciencedirect.com/topics/psychology/hedonic-adaptation.

✗ Renting an apartment or buying a house with more space than you truly need

✗ Purchasing a new phone every time a new one drops, even when your old one works just fine

✗ Shopping more for wants when you're feeling stressed or bored

✗ Joining a luxury gym or boutique fitness class you barely use

✗ Leasing a car that stretches your budget because it "feels like a reward"

✗ Regularly outsourcing things like housekeeping, pet care, or errands—not for convenience, but because you've grown used to it

None of these are inherently bad. Some might even feel like necessities based on how you've come to live. But the question is: Are you intentionally choosing these expenses, or are they simply what you've slipped into?

I like what Paula Pant says, "You can afford anything, just not everything. What's it gonna be?"[8]

From College Budget to Champagne Taste

Let's look at Sam Hill.

After four years of grinding through college and scraping by, Sam lands a well-paying job. For the first time in a long time, he feels like he can breathe. He's been driving an old beater that rattles at every stoplight. He's been skipping meals, living with roommates, and saying no to almost everything that costs money.

So, when the first paycheck hits? Sam goes all in.

He leases a brand-new SUV, gets a downtown apartment with a view, and fills it with new furniture—all on credit. And honestly? It feels great. For a while. But within a few months, that new SUV doesn't feel so new anymore. The rent that once seemed manageable now feels tight. And that credit card balance? It's creeping up too.

Sam's income went up, but his financial freedom didn't. Why? Because lifestyle creep snuck in before his long-term goals had a chance to catch up.

---

8. Paula Pant, *Afford Anything*, accessed September 3, 2025, https://affordanything.com.

It's Not About Deprivation—It's About Design

We're not here to say you should live like a college student forever. You've worked hard. You should enjoy some of your money. But the key is to do it on your terms, not on autopilot.

The danger of lifestyle creep is that it's often invisible until it's a problem. You're not suddenly living in a mansion or flying first class; it's just a hundred small decisions that keep you in the same financial place even as you earn more.

Instead, imagine this: every time your income increases, you pause and ask, *"How much of this do I want to spend, and how much do I want to save or invest?"* That simple question puts you back in control.

Lifestyle Creep Checkup

Ask yourself:

- Have your expenses increased significantly in the past year without a clear reason?
- Are you saving more now than you did last year, or just spending more?
- Do you feel like you "deserve" certain purchases after a hard day or a raise?
- Are you chasing a lifestyle you've seen on social media, rather than what matters to you?
- If you lost your job tomorrow, how long could you sustain your current lifestyle?

I am not going to tell you what you can or cannot buy. What I hope to stress upon you is that lifestyle creep will rear its ugly head in areas that you *think* you need or deserve. Awareness is the first defense. The goal isn't to eliminate joy; it's to make sure your joy doesn't come at the cost of your freedom. As you will discover later in the book, every decision you make has an opportunity cost attached to it.

> "Too many people spend money they haven't earned, to buy things they don't want, to impress people they don't like."
>
> **Will Rogers**

THE BAKER PURCHASE FACTOR:
WHY THAT $1,000 TV REALLY COSTS YOU $1,400

Have you ever heard of the Baker Purchase Factor?

Probably not, because I made it up! But once you understand it, it might change the way you look at every purchase you make.

Here's the idea:

When you buy something, whether it's a new couch, a laptop, or a giant TV, you're not just paying the sticker price. You're paying with money you *already paid taxes on*. That means you actually had to earn *more* than the price tag to afford it.

The Magic Multiplier: 1.40

Let's break it down with a real-life example.

Super Bowl Sunday is around the corner, and you decide your living room just isn't complete without a glorious 75" TV. You find one at Sam's Wholesale for $1,000 (after tax). Nice! But here's the catch . . .

In order to spend $1,000, you had to *earn* more than $1,000.

Why? Because taxes. If your combined federal and state tax rate is around 28%, then for every dollar you get to *keep*, you had to earn about $1.40.

So to buy that $1,000 TV, you actually needed to earn roughly $1,400 before taxes.

$$\$1,400 - 28\% \text{ taxes } (\$392) = \$1,008 \text{ take-home}$$

That's just enough to cover the cost of the TV.

So what's the point?

When you're shopping, try to see beyond the price tag. Multiply it by 1.4 to get the real cost in terms of what you had to earn. This applies to everything: That $50 dinner out? That's really a $70 dinner in "pre-tax" dollars. That $250 impulse buy? It took about $350 of your time and energy to earn.

It's not about guilt; it's about *awareness*.

Knowing the Baker Purchase Factor gives you one more tool to help make smarter, more intentional spending decisions. And hey—next time someone suggests a shopping spree, feel free to remind them: "You know that's 1.4 times more expensive than it looks, right?"

Ain't I fun to go shopping with?

IS EDUCATION STILL A GOOD INVESTMENT?

Ask anyone if college is worth it, and you'll probably hear one of three responses:

1. *Of course! You can't get a good job without it.*
2. *Not really—look at all the debt people are drowning in.*
3. *It depends.*

Spoiler: It depends. And the key to answering that question is understanding the concept of *return on investment*—or ROI.

We tend to treat education like it's always a guaranteed good decision, but that's no longer true across the board. With tuition costs higher than ever and student loan debt topping $1.7 trillion in the US, it's time to look at higher education for what it is: a massive financial decision. That means it deserves the same level of scrutiny and strategy as any other big investment.

What Is Education ROI, and Why Does It Matter?

ROI is a simple but powerful idea: what do you *get* for what you *give*?

When it comes to college, you're giving your time, energy, and, most importantly, money. You're also giving up earning potential during those years of study. The return? Ideally, a well-paying, stable job that uses your degree and helps you build financial independence.

If you spend $120,000 on a degree that leads to a $45,000-a-year job with limited growth, you may spend decades just trying to break even. But if you pay $45,000 for a degree that leads to an $85,000 starting salary in a high-growth industry, that's a very different story.

We're not saying your education has to *only* be about money. But ignoring financial peace is a mistake you may regret for a long time.

Degrees That Pay vs. Degrees That Don't (As Much)

Here's a simplified look at how different majors can play out financially.[9]

Major/Field	Avg. Starting Salary	20-Year ROI (Est.)	Notes
Computer Science	$75,000	$1,200,000+	High demand, strong growth
Nursing	$68,000	$850,000+	Recession-resistant, requires licensing
Business Admin	$55,000	$750,000+	Broad applicability, varies by job
Education	$42,000	$400,000–$500,000	Stable but modest pay, varies by state
English/Liberal Arts	$40,000	$250,000–$400,000	ROI increases with grad school or pivot
Performing Arts	$35,000	<$200,000	Often requires side income or gig work
Trade School (Electrician, HVAC)	$55,000	$600,000+	Low cost of entry, fast ROI

> **NOTE:** These are ballpark numbers, but they show why it's critical to match your *cost* of education with your *earning potential*.

Majoring in Strategy

Back when I was a college freshman, I really wanted to major in history. I love everything about it—the stories, the complexity, the connections across time. But I didn't come from wealth. I knew I needed a degree that would pay the bills.

So, I compromised. I majored in business administration and minored in history. But I won't lie, most of my business classes bored me to tears. However, that degree gave me the financial foundation to build a successful career.

---

9. Chart Source: Georgetown University Center on Education and the Workforce, *After Everything: Projections of Jobs, Education, and Training Requirements through 2031 – Executive Summary* (Washington, DC: Georgetown University, 2024), https://cew.georgetown.edu/wp-content/uploads/Projections2031-ES.pdf.

And that success? It's what allowed me to travel the world and feed my passion for history in real life. I've explored Petra in Jordan, gazed up at the Eiffel Tower in Paris, stood in the shadow of the Pyramids of Giza, and laid in the foxholes once occupied by Easy Company during World War II.

Degrees Aren't the Only Option Anymore

Today, traditional college is no longer the *only* path to a successful, stable career. High-paying roles are emerging in tech, trades, healthcare, and skilled labor; many of which require no college degree at all.

Some alternatives to consider:

- Trade Schools (Electrician, Plumber, HVAC Technician)
- Apprenticeships (Earn while you learn)
- Certifications (IT, Project Management, Cloud Computing, Data Analytics)
- Bootcamps (Coding, Cybersecurity, UX/UI Design)
- Entrepreneurship (Start your own thing, but be smart about it)

College is one of many tools—not the only one.

Questions to Ask Before You Commit

Before you invest tens of thousands of dollars and years of your life, pause and ask:

- Is this degree required for the job I want?
- What's the average salary in my desired field?
- Will I need grad school to be competitive?
- How much will I need to borrow—and how long will it take to pay it off?
- Are there lower-cost ways to get similar results (community college, in-state tuition, scholarships, online programs)?
- Am I pursuing this degree because I truly want to—or because I feel like I have to?

We're not anti-education. In fact, we love it. But we *are* pro-financial freedom. And the best way to protect your future is to make informed, intentional decisions today.

Invest in education when the return is worth the cost. Build a foundation first, and then, if you want to dive into your passions, you can do it from a place of strength on your own terms.

MARY CONLAN: Be Prepared for Life's Curveballs

I've spent my entire adult life working in a professional environment, never fearing job loss. I worked hard, did the right things, and believed that would always be enough. But at age 62, I was laid off due to a company restructure and younger hires replaced those of us with more experience. Competing for jobs in your 60s against candidates in their 40s is incredibly difficult. It took me six months and nearly 200 applications to finally land a great job I truly enjoy.

Thankfully, I had been saving for years and was financially stable enough to pay all my bills during that stretch. I also started an Airbnb business at age 57 that brought in about $3,000 a month. Between that income and my savings, I stayed afloat.

While job hunting, I was a finalist for three different roles. Though younger candidates were ultimately chosen, I still made the most of it. I had interviews in New York, the Virginia mountains, and Miami, and turned each trip into a mini-vacation, using airline miles and hotel points I'd saved from previous work travel. If you travel for work, I highly recommend sticking to one airline and hotel chain—those points add up quickly. I still have plenty left over for future trips.

One thing I'm grateful for is prioritizing my health. I've always exercised and taken care of myself, and at age 62, I'm often mistaken for someone in their 50s. Your appearance can matter, especially when age is so easily searchable online.

My biggest advice? Be prepared for life's unexpected turns. You're never too young to start thinking about passive income—invest early. Read self-help and personal finance books while you're young. I started too late. And remember, there's a big difference in Social Security payments at age 62 versus 70. I'm not ready to retire—I still enjoy being productive—but I also know I'm in that tricky in-between stage: too young to retire, too old to compete easily. That's why planning ahead matters.

BEING FLEXIBLE IN EDUCATION AND CAREER

We are living through one of the most transformative periods in human history. The rapid acceleration of technology, especially artificial intelligence, automation, and digital platforms, is reshaping the world of work and education. Some experts argue this change is as significant as the Industrial Revolution; others push it further, likening it to the Agricultural Revolution in terms of its scale and impact on how we live.

This is no longer a conversation about the future, because it's happening right now. From self-checkout kiosks to warehouse robots, from remote offices to AI-generated content, the way we learn, work, and earn is undergoing massive disruption. According to the *Wall Street Journal*, Walmart, the largest employer in the US, has already deployed robots to monitor inventory, clean floors, and unload trucks. That's just one example in a sea of transformation.

The COVID-19 pandemic served as a catalyst. Practically overnight, businesses of all sizes scrambled to shift to remote work, adopt digital tools, and rethink their operations. What was once unthinkable, like virtual teams, telemedicine, and digital learning, has become standard. Even the most change-resistant organizations were forced to adapt. Now, that shift is no longer temporary—it's foundational.

The implications are enormous, especially when it comes to careers and education. The truth is: the straight-line path—get a degree, land a job, work there for 40 years—is gone. Instead, we're entering the age of hybrid careers, where adaptability matters more than credentials, and where the roles of tomorrow may not even exist today.

Micro Credentialing and Lifelong Learning

In this new landscape, traditional degrees are no longer the only ticket to success. Online platforms like Coursera, Udemy, Khan Academy, and even YouTube are leveling the playing field, allowing anyone to learn valuable skills—from AI skills to graphic design to data analysis—at their own pace and expense. Employers are increasingly valuing what you can do over where you went to school.

This creates a powerful opportunity for those willing to embrace lifelong learning. You don't have to go back to college every time the world changes;

you just have to stay curious, stay current, and stay open. Microcredentials, certifications, bootcamps, and online workshops can unlock doors that a four-year degree never will.

College vs. Alternative Paths

This also means rethinking the conventional wisdom about higher education. For decades, the narrative was simple: college = success. But today, with soaring tuition costs and shifting job markets, that equation doesn't always hold. Students, and parents, need to think carefully about the return on investment. Not every degree pays off equally, and not every path requires a diploma.

Trades, apprenticeships, tech bootcamps, and entrepreneurship are legitimate, high-potential alternatives. Plumbers, electricians, and software developers may have more job security and earning potential than someone with a generic liberal arts degree and $100,000 in debt. The key is to align your education, formal or informal, with your goals and the evolving demands of the market.

Transferable Skills Are the New Currency

What you study or specialize in will always matter, but what matters even more are your *transferable skills*. These are the abilities that travel with you across industries, across roles, across life stages. Skills like communication, critical thinking, emotional intelligence, digital fluency, time management, and collaboration are becoming more valuable by the day.

When you invest in these foundational skills, you're not just preparing for a single job; you're building a toolkit for *any* job. In a world where industries rise and fall in a decade (or less), this kind of flexibility is essential.

Reinventing Yourself

One of the most important financial principles we can teach is not about money at all but about identity. The people who thrive in times of disruption are the ones who are willing to reinvent themselves. That could mean pivoting careers, returning to school, picking up new skills, or turning a hobby into a side hustle. Reinvention isn't just for rockstars or CEOs—it's for all of us.

And it doesn't have to be dramatic. You don't have to quit your job tomorrow or launch a startup. But you do need to stay aware of the changes happening around you and be willing to respond when the time comes. Whether you're 22 or 62, the mindset of adaptability will serve you far better than any single job title.

Financial Flexibility Starts with Career Flexibility

This book is about financial independence, but that journey starts long before budgeting or investing and instead begins with your ability to earn a living in a changing world. Income is the engine of wealth, and your career is the driver. If that engine stalls or becomes obsolete, you need to be able to change vehicles.

That means planning for uncertainty. It means building emergency funds, diversifying income streams, and never putting all your financial eggs in one employer's basket. It also means continuously learning and evolving, because the career you start with will probably not be the one you finish with.

Flexibility isn't just a career advantage anymore—it's a survival skill.

"College graduates spend 16 years gaining skills that will help them command a higher salary; yet little or no time is spent helping them save, invest, and grow their money."

Vince Shorb, CEO, National Financial Educators Council

Baker's Dirty Dozen

PRINCIPLE #4

Understand the Concepts of Opportunity Cost, Time Value of Money, and Compound Interest

JASON REECE: The Eighth Wonder

Albert Einstein once called compound interest "the eighth wonder of the world. He who understands it, earns it . . . he who doesn't, pays it." That might sound dramatic, but in the world of personal finance and investing, he wasn't far off.

Compound interest is the engine behind wealth building. Once you grasp just how powerful compounding can be, it becomes clear why time is the most important ingredient. The earlier you start, the less money you need to put yourself on the path to financial independence.

Thanks to a financially savvy dad, I learned this concept early. By age 14, I was already making fund selections and setting allocation percentages for my first 401(k)—yes, seriously. I was working for our family's construction company, which, unusually, offered a 401(k) plan. One day on a job site, sitting in my dad's truck, I asked, "What did Matt [my brother] pick?" My dad, usually pretty stern, replied without hesitation: "Don't worry about what he picked." That moment taught me a lot about independence, accountability, and ownership.

The most impactful lesson from that starter 401(k) came not from my own contributions, but from a monthly newsletter mailed to me in college—courtesy of my dad. In it, the investment firm managing the plan explained compound interest through charts, visuals, and a parabolic trendline that illustrated its exponential nature. But what really made it click for me was how they tied it to real life. One chart showed how a simple decision, like spending $50 today versus investing it, could grow (or disappear) over 40 years. That shift from abstract concept to concrete consequence was a game changer.

It showed me that every dollar has two lives: one spent and one invested. And the earlier you choose the latter, the more powerful the outcome becomes.

WHAT IS OPPORTUNITY COST?

Opportunity cost is one of the simplest but most powerful ideas in personal finance. It's the value of what you give up when you make a choice.

Every day you're making hundreds of these trade-offs without even thinking about them. Should I watch another episode or go to bed early? Should I buy this $7 latte every morning or invest that money? Should I take this job now or keep searching for one that aligns better with my long-term goals?

Opportunity cost isn't just about money. It shows up in our relationships, education, time, energy, and yes—our wallets. It's about understanding what you're sacrificing in every "yes" you say.

Big Financial Decisions: Si Kappa Goes to College?

Now let's look at opportunity cost as it pertains to personal finance. Take Si Kappa, a high school senior trying to decide whether to go straight into the workforce or attend college.

- **Scenario 1: Get a job right away**
  - Starting salary: $30,000/year
  - After 4 years: $120,000 earned

- **Scenario 2: Go to college**
  - Tuition and living expenses: $25,000/year → $100,000 total
  - Lost wages from not working: $120,000
  - Opportunity Cost of College = **$220,000**

At first glance, it might seem like skipping college is the smart financial move. But here's the twist: studies consistently show that people with college degrees typically earn more, often double, over their lifetimes compared to those without.

So Si's opportunity cost might pay off in the long run. But he needs to know the full cost; not just tuition but also what he's giving up to make an informed decision.

Baker Canon: The Water Rule

From day one, my wife and I had a rule whenever we ate out with our daughters: everyone drinks water. Why? Because we told them that saving on drinks now would help us pay for their college later.

One day, when our daughters were about three and five, a waiter asked what they wanted to drink. Without hesitation, our eldest said, "I want water because I want to go to college!" The younger one followed suit, "Me want water! Wanna go college!"

The waiter looked confused, but I didn't even try to explain.

Now, let's do the math for the real cost of that drink:[1]

- 4 people x 3 meals out/week = 12 drinks
- $3 per drink = $36/week
- $36/week = $1,872/year

Let's say you invested that $36/week instead, in a low-cost index fund with 8% annual returns:

- After 10 years = $27,000
- After 17 years = $63,000
- After 30 years = $212,000

That's college money. That's a down payment on a house. That's retirement savings. All hidden in the cost of soda and sweet tea.

Now take a single example. A relative recently ordered a cocktail with dinner:

- Cost: $12
- Local city alcohol tax: 30% → $3.60
- Tip: $2.40
- Total: $18

---

1. Calculations were made on my trusty Texas Instruments BA-35 Financial Calculator. Old School!

And when you apply the Baker Purchase Factor of 1.40 (because it's post-tax income), the real cost was $25.

Opportunity cost isn't always a college vs. no college decision. Sometimes it's just, "Do I really need this cocktail at dinner, or is it costing me more than it's worth?"

Modern Life, Modern Opportunity Costs

In today's world, opportunity cost shows up in newer ways too:

- **Streaming vs. Skill-building:** That time spent binge-watching a show could be used to learn graphic design, coding, or start a side hustle.
- **Buying the Latest Tech vs. Investing:** That $1,200 phone every year could be $10,000 in your investment account in a decade.
- **Lifestyle Creep:** Every raise you absorb into your lifestyle instead of investing delays your financial independence.

The point isn't to guilt you into drinking water or canceling Netflix. It's to recognize that every choice has a trade-off, and the more aware you are of them, the more power you have over your financial future.

INFLATION

Years ago, one of my daughters had a pocket full of pennies. Tired of carrying them, she decided to dump the whole handful on the pavement. When her mom caught her in the act, she was not amused and made her crawl under the car to pick up every single one.

My daughter didn't understand what all the fuss was about. After all, what's a penny even worth anymore? And honestly, she's not wrong. Today, it costs the US government more to make a penny than the penny is worth.

But a hundred years ago? Those few copper coins could buy something. That's inflation. Over time, money loses value. What bought a meal back then barely buys a stick of gum now. It's not just about pennies; it's about understanding that the same dollar in your hand today will almost certainly be worth less tomorrow. But there is another financial concept that can take on inflation. Enter: The Time Value of Money.

Time Is Literally Money

The Time Value of Money (TVM) is the idea that a dollar in your hand today is worth *more* than the same dollar in the future. Why? Because money now can be *invested*, *used*, or *saved*—and while it's just sitting there, it's either growing—or losing—buying power due to inflation.

Here's the simplest way to put it:

If cousin Eddie owes you $1,000 and says, "I can give it to you today or one year from now," what should you say?

Take the money today. Why? Because in a year, that same $1,000 may not be able to buy as much. Worse—if you had invested it now, it could've already earned a return.

That's the power of *present value* vs. *future value*. The earlier you have money, the more potential it has to grow.

What Is Compound Interest?

Now here's where things really take off: Compound interest is the engine that turns time into wealth.

Compound interest is when you earn interest on your interest. It means that not only is your original investment growing, but your *growth is growing* too.

Here's the formal definition:

"Compound interest is interest calculated on the initial principal, which also includes all the accumulated interest from previous periods."[2]

The takeaway? Time + compound interest = magic. That's why starting early is one of the most powerful moves in personal finance.

The Power of Starting Early

Let's look at three investors all putting in the same amount of money but starting at different times.

---

2. Julia Kagan, "Compound Interest," *Investopedia*, November 9, 2020, https://www.investopedia.com/terms/c/compoundinterest.asp.

Sally May, Moe Skeeto, and Luna Tick

Saver	Amount Invested	Age Invested	Ending Balance at Age 60
Sally May	$30,000	25–35	$297,635
Moe Skeeto	$30,000	35–45	$151,511
Luna Tick	$30,000	45–55	$68,140

All three invested the same amount—$250 per month for 10 years, totaling $30,000 each. Assuming an 8% annual return compounded monthly, Sally ended up with nearly five times more than Luna.[3]

Why? Time. Sally's money had more time to compound. That's the only difference.

This is why one of my biggest financial regrets is not investing more in my early years. Back then, retirement felt a million miles away. But today, I know that starting even a *little* earlier makes a massive difference in the long run.

A Quick Word on Negative Compound Interest

Compound interest works both ways. Just like your investments can grow exponentially, so can your debt.

Carrying a credit card balance with a 20% interest rate? That's compound interest *working against you*. What starts as a manageable balance quickly snowballs into a debt trap.

Compound interest is a powerful force. Use it to your advantage, not your downfall.

SO, YOU WANT TO BE A MILLIONAIRE?

Millionaire status isn't reserved for celebrities, lottery winners, or crypto bros. In fact, it's more achievable than ever, and far more common than most people realize.

According to 2023 estimates from Credit Suisse and other sources, about 23.7 million US households now have a net worth of $1 million or

---

3. Calculated using the Compound Interest Calculator at Bankrate.com, https://www.bankrate.com/banking /savings/compound-savings-calculator/.

more. That's roughly 18% of all households. And the number keeps growing. In 2024 alone, an additional 560,000 people crossed the millionaire mark, according to a report from investment bank UBS.

You might be wondering, "Who are all these millionaires? I sure don't see them." That's because most millionaires don't typically flaunt their wealth. They are not driving flashy cars or living in mansions. In fact, they are often hiding in plain sight. Think of the scrap iron dealer down the road, the woman who runs the local pawn shop, or the plumbing contractor who has been quietly building wealth one job at a time.[4]

So what gives? How did these "invisible millionaires" get there? And more importantly, how can you?

Let's Talk About What a Millionaire *Really* Is

It's important to clarify: when we say *millionaire*, we're talking about net worth—which means all your assets minus all your liabilities.

That includes:

- Retirement accounts (401(k), IRA)
- Home equity
- Brokerage investments
- Cash savings
- Business equity
- And yes, even your used Honda Civic

However, in this book, we like to zoom in on something even more powerful than raw net worth: liquid net assets. These are the accounts you can access and manage today such as your savings, investments, and retirement funds. That's the kind of wealth that moves with you and gives you real control.

---

4. UBS, Global Wealth Report 2023, Zurich: *UBS* Group AG, August 15, 2023, https://www.ubs.com/global/en /media/display-page-ndp/en-20230815-global-wealth-report-2023.html.

Myth-Busting Millionaire Stats

- 79% of millionaires received *zero inheritance.*
- 8 out of 10 invest consistently in their company's 401(k).
- Only 31% averaged $100k or more a year.
- 1 in 3 never earned six figures in a single year.
- Top 5 careers? Engineer, accountant, teacher, manager, attorney.

Let that sink in. You don't need a trust fund, tech startup, or explosive income. You just need a plan.

Most millionaires don't "look" rich. They don't live in mansions or drive Teslas. In fact, the typical American millionaire is more like your neighbor across the street with a modest truck and a paid-off house. Coming from a family of teachers, it's encouraging to know that reaching millionaire status is not only possible, but well within reach.

Dr. Thomas J. Stanley and William D. Danko's *The Millionaire Next Door*[5] broke it down after 20 years of research:

- They are self-employed, frugal, hard-working, invests 20% of their income, and live well below their means.
- Their partner is the household CFO—planning, budgeting, saving.
- They spend heavily on their children's education and make their own investment decisions.

That was the portrait of a millionaire in the '90s. And while those principles still hold, the picture is evolving.

The Tide of Change: A New Generation of Millionaires

Let's be real: the millionaire mold is breaking.

Today, you're just as likely to meet a millionaire who's a single woman, a teacher with a Roth IRA, a freelancer with index funds, or a dual-income couple who never upgraded their lifestyle with every raise.

Gender roles, cultural expectations, and career paths are shifting, and so is the path to wealth. The new millionaire doesn't fit a single profile, and that's good news for everyone.

---

5. See Thomas J. Stanley and William D. Danko, *The Millionaire Next Door* (New York: Pocket Books, 1986), https://themillionairenextdoor.com.

Because that means millionaire status is about *what you do*, not *who you are*.

Speaking of "who you are" most people think that all doctors are millionaires. Right now, 24% of doctors in their 60s still aren't millionaires, despite decades of high income.[6]

5 Key Lessons from Millionaires

Whether we're looking at the old school millionaires or the new generation building quiet wealth, the same timeless truths apply:

1. **Education Is an Investment.** Not just degrees, but financial literacy passed down from generation to generation. Most times, I will inscribe in my books, "Invest in knowledge."
2. **Budgeting Is Power**. Someone in the household has to know where the money goes and steer the ship.
3. **Kids Don't Break the Bank**. With discipline and planning, families can build wealth, too.
4. **Work-Life Balance Is Possible**. Millionaires work hard, but they don't always work themselves to death.
5. **Frugality + Consistent Investing = Wealth**. Living below your means and investing early and often is the magic formula.

You don't have to start with a huge salary, inheritance, or a flashy business idea.

You just need a consistent plan and a willingness to stick to it over time.

If you're serious about becoming a millionaire, there's no better place to start than with Baker's Dirty Dozen Principle #8.

Start now. Invest consistently. Stay the course.

---

6. Jim Dahle, "Are Doctors Millionaires? The Truth About the Average Doctor Net Worth," *The White Coat Investor*, July 17, 2020, https://www.whitecoatinvestor.com/physician-millionaires/.

PRINCIPLE #5

Boom or Budget: Navigating Financial Minefields Without Losing a Limb

In a world where you can buy a couch at 2 a.m. with one click (and maybe Crumbl cookies while you're at it), keeping track of how and why you spend your money has never been more important. Every generation, from TikTok teens to boomer grandparents, has its own unique relationship with money, shaped by the times they've lived through and the tech in their pockets. By digging into these generational quirks, we can spot the common traps, laugh at a few habits (ours and others'), and most importantly, learn how to steer clear of the financial minefields that trip up even the savviest spender.

GENERATION Z (BORN 1997–2012): THE DIGITAL NATIVES

- **Spending Power**: Gen Z's annual spending is projected to reach $360 billion in the US alone, with expectations to account for 25–30% of all luxury purchases by 2030.[1]
- **Influence of Social Media**: Approximately 71% of Gen Z discovers new products through social media platforms, making them highly susceptible to influencer marketing.[2]

---

1. "How can brands capture the loyalty of Gen Z?" *Vogue Business*, February 21, 2025, https://www.voguebusiness.com/story/consumers/how-can-brands-capture-the-loyalty-of-gen-z.
2. Josh Howarth, "85+ Stats on Gen Z Spending and Buying Habits (2025)," *Exploding Topics*, June 5, 2025, https://explodingtopics.com/blog/gen-z-spending.

- **Value-Driven Purchases**: A significant number are more likely to buy from companies that treat their employees well, and most prefer brands that align with their personal values.
- **Financial Behavior**: Despite their spending power, nearly half of Gen Zers rely on financial assistance from their parents, highlighting the importance of financial education and budgeting.[3]

Financial Minefield: *The ease of online shopping and the influence of social media can lead to impulsive spending.*

Strategy: *Implementing budgeting tools and setting clear financial goals can help mitigate unnecessary expenditures.*

MILLENNIALS (BORN 1981-1996): THE PURPOSEFUL SPENDERS

- **Annual Expenditure**: Millennials have an estimated annual spending of $3–4 trillion, making them a significant economic force.[4]
- **Conscious Consumption**: A notable 75% prioritize sustainability in their purchases, and 62% favor products that reflect their political and social beliefs.[5]
- **Digital Savvy**: Millennials extensively research products online before purchasing, with 80% reading reviews to ensure value for money.

Financial Minefield: *The desire to support ethical brands can sometimes lead to higher spending.*

Strategy: *Balancing values with budget constraints by seeking affordable ethical alternatives can maintain financial health.*

3. Chantelle Lee, "'We Want to Be Independent': Nearly Half of Gen Zers Rely on Financial Help From Parents," *TIME*, July 17, 2024, https://time.com/6999832/gen-z-financial-help-parents-bank-of-america-report/.
4. "Consumer Shopping Trends and Statistics by the Generation," Porch Group Media, July 10, 2024, https://porchgroupmedia.com/blog/generational-consumer-shopping-trends/.
5. "Millennial spending habits: Budget minded, socially conscious," *The Future of Commerce*, June 17, 2024, https://www.the-future-of-commerce.com/2024/06/17/millennial-spending-habits/.

GENERATION X (BORN 1965-1980): THE CAUTIOUS CONSUMERS

- **Financial Responsibilities**: Gen Xers often juggle multiple financial obligations, including mortgages, education expenses, and caring for aging parents.
- **Debt Levels**: Surprisingly, they carry the highest average debt among generations, averaging around $61,000 per household.[6]
- **Spending Habits**: Over half have cut back on discretionary spending due to economic uncertainties, and 27% have less than $1,000 in savings.[7]

Financial Minefield: *Balancing current expenses with long-term savings can be challenging.*

Strategy: *Prioritizing debt reduction and building an emergency fund can provide financial stability.*

BABY BOOMERS (BORN 1946-1964): THE TRADITIONALISTS

- **Wealth Status**: Baby Boomers hold a significant portion of the nation's wealth, with many enjoying financial security in retirement.
- **Spending Preferences**: They tend to spend on travel, health, and wellness, often booking vacations impulsively and investing in self-care.[8]

---

6. "Generation X: Years, stats, work, spending trends," *The Future of Commerce*, November 1, 2023, https://www.the-future-of-commerce.com/2023/11/01/generation-x-definition-years-stats-work-spending-trends/.

7. "Generational Spending Habits: How Gen X, Z and Millennials Compare," *First Merchants Bank*, December 23, 2024, https://www.firstmerchants.com/resources/learn/blogs/blog-detail/resource-library/2024/12/23/generational-spending-habits--how-gen-x--z-and-millennials-compare?.

8. Stephanie Harlow, "Baby Boomers Spending Habits: Trends Shaping 2025 Consumer Behavior," *GWI*, accessed September 17, 2025, https://www.gwi.com/blog/baby-boomers-spending-habits.

- **Digital Adoption**: While traditionally favoring in-person shopping, there's a growing trend of Boomers making digital purchases, adapting to modern conveniences.

Financial Minefield: *Today's financial minefield includes a growing number of online scams specifically targeting older adults. Fraudsters prey on trust and unfamiliarity with digital tools, making retirees especially vulnerable.*

Strategy: *Staying educated about common scam tactics, like phishing emails, fake investment opportunities, and fraudulent tech support calls, can protect your hard-earned nest egg from disappearing with a single click.*

WRAPPING IT UP

Every generation has its own money quirks, whether it's boomers clinging to landlines or Gen Z investing in crypto and coffee at the same time. But when you understand the habits that shape your spending, you can spot the traps before you fall into them. Recognizing these patterns isn't about blame, it's about building smarter strategies that actually fit your life. That's how you avoid the financial landmines and start paving your own road to long-term independence.

The other day, I realized my wife's 2011 Highlander needed new windshield wiper blades. That tiny task somehow spiraled into a full-blown thought experiment: *How would each generation go about buying wiper blades?*

Gen Z: "Hey, Mom, should there be any rubber on my wipers?"

Gen X Mom: "Yes, sweetie."

Gen Z: "I def need some new ones then."

Gen X Dad: "Anything you want, we will get, but we need to find some that are the highest quality."

Gen Z: "Cool. I saw a wiper blade hack on TikTok and know the best ones to get."

Millennials: Googles: "best environmentally friendly windshield wiper blades 2025." Spends two hours reading reviews, comparing brands, and watching three YouTube videos before finally ordering online. Then Googles: "how to install windshield wipers without crying."

Gen X: "I trust Wiper City. They've always treated me right." Checks online, confirms they still exist, drives there. Leaves with the premium model, warranty plan, and a free air freshener.

Boomers: Joe to Brenda: "You need wipers? I'll head down to Wiper Blades & More and talk to Burt." Greets with a handshake, buys the best set they sell, pays twice as much, and tips the guy for installing them in the rain.

Silent Generation: Grandpa: "I'm getting new wipers for the '62 pickup." Grandma: "They stopped making those in 1987. Just call our granddaughter—she'll get 'em off the Google."

FINANCIAL MINEFIELDS

Weddings

Cue the music, cue the tears, cue the credit card bills.

You've been dreaming of this day your whole life. You booked the venue a year ago. You survived the showers, the tastings, the dress fittings, the Pinterest boards, the bachelorette/bachelor extravaganza in Nashville (because it's always Nashville), and now . . . it's *go time*.

Your vows say, "for richer or poorer," but your bank account didn't think that would kick in *before* the honeymoon.

Let's be honest: the wedding industry has become a well-oiled, wildly expensive machine. You're not just planning a celebration; you're expected to throw a full-scale theatrical production with drone footage and a signature cocktail named after your dog.

The Numbers: Yikes!

According to *The Knot's* 2023 Real Weddings Study:[9]

- Average cost of a US wedding (excluding honeymoon): $30,000
- Venue: $11,200
- Catering: $75/person
- Photography: $2,600
- Flowers: $2,400
- Reception Band or DJ: $1,500–$4,000
- Wedding Dress: $1,900
- Average guest count: 117

Prices skyrocket in places like Manhattan, where the average wedding hits a jaw-dropping $78,000. Meanwhile, if you're open to a scenic ceremony in Arkansas or South Dakota, you might pull it off for under $20,000.

Reality Check: What Are You *Really* Paying For?

You're not just paying for a meal and some nice pictures. You're also buying into expectations. And often, those expectations are driven by filtered Instagram posts, viral proposal videos, and one-upmanship that's turned the "best day of your life" into a very expensive performance.

If you're feeling this pressure, you're not alone, and you're not a cynic for questioning it.

So maybe, just maybe, there's another way.

The Case for Eloping (Hear Me Out)

- ✓ You'll save serious cash.
- ✓ You'll save your sanity.
- ✓ Your friends won't be forced to spend $200 to wear matching suits/dresses they'll never wear again.
- ✓ You'll remember the honeymoon more than the color of your napkins anyway.
- ✓ You can still throw a blowout party later—on your terms.

---

9. "The Knot 2023 Real Weddings Study," *The Knot*, February 26, 2025, https://www.theknot.com/content/wedding-data-insights/weddings-in-2023.

One couple we know skipped the big wedding and hosted a backyard ceremony followed by a dance party at an old train station. They came in under budget, took a killer honeymoon, and still had money left over for grad school. That's what we call a wedding win. A win for me, because it just so happened to be my daughter.

If You're Going Traditional—Here's How to Keep It Smart

- Ask friends or family to help with decor, bartending, or music.
- Borrow instead of buy—plenty of people have glassware and vases collecting dust in a garage.
- Have a talented friend take the photos or video.
- Choose an off-season or weekday date for venue discounts.
- Shrink your guest list. (Yes, Aunt Marge's cousin from Toledo will survive not being invited.)
- Shop around and negotiate. Vendors expect it.
- Create a budget and offer an incentive to stick to it. (We told our daughter and her fiancé: "Here's $ *set amount*—whatever you don't spend, you keep." Worked like a charm.)

Opportunity Cost: The Wedding That Could Fund Your Future

Let's say you dial your wedding budget back from $34,000 to $16,000. That's $18,000 in potential savings.

If you invest that savings—say $9,000 each into your 401(k)s with an 8% return—here's what that looks like:

- After 10 years: $19,977 each
- After 20 years: $44,341 each
- After 30 years: $98,422 each

That's almost $200,000 for your future. All for trimming a few guest list names and skipping the live flamingo release.[10]

---

10. Calculated using the Compound Interest Calculator at Bankrate.com, https://www.bankrate.com/banking /savings/compound-savings-calculator/.

SCOTT NAEGER: Wedding Budget Gone Wild!

Here's a cautionary tale for any parent getting ready to marry off a daughter: set a wedding budget and stick to it like your retirement depends on it. Because it just might.

Almost 20 years ago, my oldest daughter, who was 22 at the time, came to my wife and me with the big announcement—she was getting married. The wedding was set for 18 months out, which I thought gave us plenty of time to plan and save. We agreed on a reasonable budget of $10,000. That was the plan. Spoiler alert: it did not go according to plan.

Her fiancé came from a family with a much higher income than ours and he came with a list of "ideas" that were what I'll politely call *budget busters*. He wanted a picturesque ceremony in Forest Park, a swanky downtown St. Louis reception, and every trendy wedding feature you could think of.

As months went by, the "small upgrades" kept piling up. My wife and daughter, fueled by Pinterest dreams and bridal magazine inspiration, kept coming to me with "just one more thing." The budget crept from $10,000 to $13,000 . . . then to $15,000. That's when I drew the line: no more. Fifteen thousand. Final offer.

So what did they do? They set me up.

They scheduled a visit to "just take a look" at the upscale venue downtown. The four of them—my daughter, her fiancé, my wife, and his mother—ganged up on me. I didn't stand a chance. I walked into that place thinking I was the financial gatekeeper . . . and walked out $7,000 deeper in the hole.

By the end, we'd spent over $22,000—roughly $36,000 in today's money. And here's the kicker: the marriage only lasted four years.

If I could offer one piece of advice to fellow dads out there: set a budget, put that amount in a separate account, and make it clear that when it's gone, it's gone. No extensions, no upgrades, no exceptions. Guard that line like your 401(k) depends on it. Because it does. And yes, your wife and daughter may be temporarily devastated . . . but your bank account will thank you.

Funerals

Losing a loved one is emotionally devastating. Unfortunately, it can also be financially overwhelming. During such times, families should focus on grieving and honoring the deceased, not on navigating unexpected expenses. Yet the reality is that funeral costs can be a significant burden if not planned for in advance.

According to the National Funeral Directors Association (NFDA), the median cost of a funeral with a viewing and burial in 2023 was $8,300, while the median cost for a funeral with cremation was $6,280. These figures do not include additional expenses such as cemetery plots, headstones, flowers, or obituaries.[11]

Strategies to Mitigate Funeral Expenses

1. Consider Cremation Over Traditional Burial

Cremation is generally less expensive than traditional burial. Opting for cremation can save thousands of dollars, especially when forgoing services like embalming or elaborate caskets. My own wishes, including the instructions I've shared with loved ones, are to be cremated, with my ashes placed in a Living Urn and planted as a tree at Baker's Acres, our family farm in southern Arkansas. Knowing my family, it will likely be a persimmon tree.[12]

Whatever you choose, be sure your final wishes are clearly documented and included in your estate planning.

2. Plan Ahead and Document Wishes

Clearly outlining your funeral preferences can alleviate stress for your loved ones and prevent unnecessary expenditures. Whether you prefer cremation, donation to science, or a traditional burial, documenting your wishes ensures they are honored.

---

11. National Funeral Directors Association, *Statistics*, last updated September 24, 2024, https://nfda.org/news/statistics.
12. The Living Urn, *Urns for Ashes | Tree Burial & Cremation Urns*, accessed September 3, 2025, https://www.thelivingurn.com.

3. Decline Unnecessary Add-Ons

Be cautious of upselling tactics that may pressure you into purchasing unnecessary items, such as gasketed caskets or elaborate embalming services. Remember, the value of a funeral lies in the remembrance, not the price tag.

4. Shop Around and Compare Prices

Funeral homes are required by law to provide a General Price List (GPL) upon request.[13] Take the time to compare prices and services from multiple providers to ensure you're making informed decisions.

5. Explore Body Donation to Science

Both of my parents chose to donate their bodies to the Louisiana State University (LSU) Medical School in Shreveport, LA. My father passed away in 2007 and my mother in 2009. After their passing, we contacted LSU-Shreveport, which had been prearranged through a simple one-page agreement, and they came to the hospital to receive their remains.

The medical school kept their bodies for about a year before returning the cremated remains to me. In each case, we held a memorial service at our local church soon after their passing. Once we received their ashes, we laid them to rest in the family cemetery.

It's a uniquely meaningful act—to continue giving, even after death.

Final Thoughts on End of Life

Planning for end-of-life expenses is a sensitive but necessary aspect of financial preparedness. By taking proactive steps, you can ensure that your final wishes are respected and that your loved ones are not burdened with unexpected costs during their time of grief.

"Principle #11: Protect Your Assets" dives into some of the most dangerous financial minefields—divorce, investment fraud, identity theft, and more. Any one of them can blast a crater in your net worth if you're not paying attention.

---

13. Federal Trade Commission, *Funeral Rule*, last updated September 24, 2024, https://www.ftc.gov/news-events/topics/truth-advertising/funeral-rule.

KEEP CALM AND BUDGET

Let's clear the air: "budgeting" might be one of the most misunderstood words in personal finance. It sounds restrictive. It feels like punishment. And if you're anything like I used to be, you probably thought budgeting was only for people barely scraping by or those buried under a mountain of credit card debt.

Spoiler alert: it's not.

Whether you're making six figures or trying to figure out how to make rent, everyone needs to know where their money is going. Because if you don't tell your dollars where to go, they'll wander off—and good luck finding them later.

Budgeting isn't about guilt or deprivation. It's about clarity. Control. Confidence. It's about giving yourself permission to spend *with purpose,* not panic.

And believe it or not, it can feel pretty euphoric to organize your finances and actually hit your goals. There's a surprising high in seeing that little "amount saved" number grow, even if it's just from cutting your daily coffee habit in half.

Want to terrify yourself into action? Go back through the last 90 days of spending and categorize every single purchase. You may discover that the $7 lattes, Friday night takeout, and impulse Amazon buys have quietly siphoned off more than you'd care to admit. Death by a thousand $12.99 subscriptions.

But here's the good news: budgeting doesn't have to be complicated, rigid, or miserable. There are a dozen ways to track your money, and the best one is whichever one you'll *actually stick with.* Your lifestyle, your personality, your rules.

At the end of the day, the only *real* rule of budgeting is this: Don't spend more than you make.

If you're already fairly savvy with your finances and keep a general mental tab of your spending, then a simple monthly budget might be all you need to polish things up. For others, it might mean starting from scratch with a more hands-on approach: apps, budget envelopes, physical planners—whatever helps you take ownership.

Because budgeting isn't just about saying "no." It's about being able to say "yes" to the things that *actually matter.*

Budgeting Plans: Pick Your Money Map

By now, hopefully you're starting to believe that budgeting isn't some cruel punishment for people who overspend but rather a smart move for *everyone* who wants to reach financial independence. But here's the thing: there's no one-size-fits-all method. Different personalities, goals, and lifestyles call for different plans.

Think of budgeting like choosing a GPS: some give you turn-by-turn directions (down to the dollar), and others just keep you generally headed in the right direction. Let's explore two of the most popular, and effective, approaches.

Option 1: Zero-Based Budgeting
For the detail-oriented, goal-driven budgeter

If you're ready to take control of every dollar and put your spending on lockdown, zero-based budgeting is for you. The idea is simple: assign *every* single dollar you earn to a specific job until there's nothing left unaccounted for. You're aiming for your income minus expenses to equal . . . zero.

Think of it as a game of money Tetris—every block has a place, and you win when everything fits perfectly.

How It Works

Step 1: Know Your Take-Home Pay

This is your income after taxes, health premiums, 401(k) contributions, etc.—what actually hits your bank account.

Step 2: Cover the Essentials

Rent or mortgage, utilities, groceries, transportation, insurance, and debt minimums. You can also include charitable giving if that's part of your plan.

Step 3: Plan for Discretionary Expenses

Dining out, entertainment, travel, subscriptions—anything non-essential. Be honest here. This is where your budget can spring leaks.

Step 4: Calculate What's Left

Take-home pay minus steps 2 and 3 = your disposable income.

Step 5: Assign Your Disposable Income to Goals

Emergency fund? Down payment on a house? Paying down credit card debt? Investing for retirement? Allocate the remainder here. When you're done, your balance should be $0.

> **Tip:** If your goals don't fit with what's left over, revisit the "wants" and trim some fat.

Best for: *People with debt, ambitious savings goals, or who need detailed oversight.*

Commitment level: *High. This method takes focus, but the results can be powerful.[14]*

Option 2: The 50/30/20 Plan[15]

For the laid-back budgeter who still wants structure

Popularized by Senator Elizabeth Warren in *All Your Worth: The Ultimate Money Plan*,[16] this is a simple and flexible method that divides your take-home pay into three broad categories. No spreadsheets, no micromanaging—just a clean framework to guide your spending.

Think of it like slicing your income pie into three manageable pieces.

How It Works

Step 1: Know Your Take-Home Pay

What you actually bring home after deductions.

Step 2: Look at Past Spending

Review your last 2–3 months of expenses. Grab your bank statements and brace yourself—this step is eye-opening.

14. "5 Steps to Creating Your Best Budget," *Your Financial Pharmacist,* January 11, 2018, https://yourfinancial pharmacist.com/5-steps-to-creating-your-best-budget/.

15. Elizabeth Warren and Amelia Warren Tyagi, *All Your Worth: The Ultimate Lifetime Money Plan* (New York: Free Press, 2005).

16. Opher Ganel, "Why the '50/30/20 Rule' Proposed by Elizabeth Warren Can Hurt Your Finances," *Wealthtender,* March 31, 2023, https://wealthtender.com/insights/money-management/avoid-using-elizabeth-warrens -proposed-personal-budget-plan.

Step 3: Divide It Up

- **50% → Needs:** Rent/mortgage, groceries, gas, insurance, utilities, minimum loan payments. If you're over 50%, it may be time to adjust your lifestyle (or your zip code).
- **30% → Wants** *(we'd argue for 25%)*: Dining out, hobbies, travel, streaming services, premium upgrades. This is your lifestyle spending, but it can easily balloon into "lifestyle creep."
- **20% → Savings and Debt Paydown** *(we'd also argue for 25%)*: Emergency fund, 401(k), Roth IRA, extra payments on loans—anything that builds your future.

Step 4: Track and Adjust

This isn't a set-it-and-forget-it plan. Income and expenses change so your budget should flex with them.

Best for: *Beginners, folks with low debt, or anyone who wants a simple, effective structure.*

Commitment level: *Moderate. Less precise than zero-based, but far easier to maintain.*

The truth is, no budget is perfect, but any budget is better than no budget. So whether you choose a precision tool or a broader framework, the key is to stay consistent and keep tweaking until it works for *you*.

If you run into difficulty in cutting expenses to achieve your financial goals, then examine the income side of the equation. Are there ways to increase your income with a side hustle or maybe even get a higher paying job?

When I downsized, I bought the cutest little house, and tucked away in the back-yard was an even smaller house. It was run down, with vines crawling up the sides and drafty old single-pane windows. The previous owner had used it for storage, but one of my neighbors told me it had a livelier past. Apparently, it was the original Man Cave in Marietta, where the guys used to gather to play cards.

I decided to give it new life as a She Shed.

I spruced it up, gave it a charming makeover, and did some landscaping to make the backyard feel welcoming. It turned out beautifully. But after a while, I realized I wasn't using it much. That's when the lightbulb went off: Airbnb.

I listed the cottage and—bank! It started paying for the mortgage, the utilities, and even gave me enough extra to make improvements on the main house. That little backyard bonus became a steady stream of passive income.

If you've got vision and an eye for potential, I say go for it. With a little effort, you could turn something forgotten into something that pays for itself, and then some. Passive income? Try free house!

RESOURCES FOR BUDGETING: FIND WHAT WORKS FOR YOU

Budgeting doesn't need to be complicated, but it does need to be consistent and that's where the right tools come in. Whether you're a tech-lover or some-one who prefers the envelope method, the key is to find a system that fits *you*.

Here are some go-to tools that can make managing your money easier, smarter, and more intuitive.

Easy-to-Use Budgeting Apps

There are more budgeting apps than ever, but a few stand out for their fea-tures, ease of use, and ability to keep your money organized. These are solid options to explore:

- **YNAB (You Need a Budget):** A powerhouse for zero-based budgeting. Helps you assign every dollar, track in real time, and plan ahead. Great for detail lovers and goal crushers.

- **EveryDollar:** Created by Dave Ramsey's team. Based on zero-based budgeting principles but with a very simple interface which is great for beginners or folks who want fast setup.
- **Rocket Money (formerly Truebill):** Helps you monitor subscriptions, cancel unused services, and optimize bills. A good choice for people who want automation with less math.
- **PocketGuard:** Tells you how much "spendable" money you have after bills and goals. Visually appealing and great for people who like quick snapshots of their budget health.
- **NerdWallet:** Tracks spending while offering loads of educational content. Best for people who want a little financial coaching along the way.
- **Goodbudget:** A digital take on the envelope method. You set spending categories and "fund" them—perfect for couples and cash-style thinkers.
- **Monarch Money** and **Copilot:** Both apps are gaining popularity for users wanting an all-in-one finance dashboard.

Budget Envelopes: The Power of Cash

Sometimes the best tool doesn't involve technology at all. Budgeting envelopes are a classic, tactile way to control spending, especially for problem areas like eating out, impulse buys, or entertainment. A set amount of cash goes into individual envelopes labeled for categories like gas, groceries, fun, or whatever fits your budget plan. You can customize the labels however you like to reflect your spending priorities.

There's just something about handing over physical cash that makes you *think* before spending. If you struggle with swiping a card too often, this might be your best move.

- Use envelopes for your full budget or just for certain categories.
- You can buy custom envelopes online (check Etsy), or DIY them at home.
- This is a great method for those who want to physically *feel* their money and need structure without screens.

Apps for Splitting Expenses: Keeping It Fair with Friends

Budgeting often involves other people like roommates, travel buddies, and partners. These apps keep everything above board and drama-free:

- **Venmo / Cash App / PayPal / Zelle**: Quick peer-to-peer transfers for splitting rent, bills, or pizza.
- **Splitwise / Splittr**: Awesome for group travel, shared expenses, or recurring costs. No more "who paid for what again?" arguments.

> **BAKER'S TIP:** Apps like Splitwise have saved many a road trip and friend group. Fairness is financial harmony, and technology makes it painless.

DR. BLAKE TORRES, PHARMD: Running on Empty (Literally)

Back in pharmacy school when I was young, broke, and blissfully married (still am), my wife and I lived in a two-bedroom house with one bathroom, a chocolate lab, and zero dollars to spare. She was a schoolteacher, I was a full-time student, and our combined income could barely keep the lights on, much less fill a gas tank.

One morning, she'd already left for work, and I was heading out early for an exam. I got in the car, turned the key, and saw the dreaded "E." I figured I could maybe coast 10 miles to the gas station. I checked the bank account: negative balance. Credit card? Maxed out. Payday? Tomorrow.

I launched a full-blown coin hunt through drawers, pockets, couch cushions. Nothing. I even eyed the dog's treat jar in desperation. Then, a light bulb: our $3 AT&T roadside assistance plan. I vaguely remembered it included 3 gallons of emergency gas. One phone call later, a guy showed up at our driveway and filled the tank. Crisis averted.

I don't remember if I aced the test, but I never forgot the real lesson: be prepared. Since then, we've kept a $20 bill hidden in each car because you never know when your next great financial strategy will involve a telecom company and a red gas can.

SHOULD I INCLUDE AN EMERGENCY FUND IN MY BUDGET?

Short answer? Yes. 100%. Absolutely.

So, how much should you save?

The general recommendation is to have three to six months' worth of expenses set aside. Enough to cover your rent or mortgage, food, utilities, gas, insurance, and everything you'd need to stay afloat if you lost your income temporarily.

Now, I know what some of you are thinking: *"That's nice . . . but I have student loans, childcare costs, and a job that barely stretches as it is."*

Totally fair. For many young professionals, saving that much might feel impossible. But don't let that stop you from starting. Every small bit helps.

Start Small. Build Fast.

1. **Track your spending for a few months.**
   Get a real picture of your monthly baseline and not just what you think you spend.

2. **Set a mini-goal.**
   Maybe it's $500 to start. Then $1,000. Then one month's expenses. Progress is more important than perfection.

3. **Keep it accessible but separate.**
   Store your emergency fund in a high-yield savings account or money market account—not your checking account. You want it safe, liquid, and *not too easy* to dip into for concert tickets.

Why It Matters

Emergencies don't wait for you to be "ready." Car trouble, a broken appliance, job loss, or a surprise medical bill can undo years of financial progress. An emergency fund gives you options. Breathing room. Peace of mind.

And when the storm passes (because it will), you won't be starting over; you'll be standing strong.

Negotiate Almost Anything

As my dad always told me: "It's not how much you make—it's how much you keep." One of the best ways to *keep* more of your hard-earned cash? Ask for a better deal. Seriously! Just ask.

Negotiation isn't just for buying cars or closing business deals. It's a mindset. It's about *advocating for yourself*, whether it's trimming $15 off your cell phone bill or knocking $500 off a medical charge.

And over the years, I've negotiated just about everything, from satellite radio subscriptions to hotel rooms and even college tuition. Here's what I've learned (often to the mild embarrassment of my daughters): most prices aren't set in stone.

Let's walk through some of the best, and most overlooked, opportunities to negotiate and save.

Medical Bills: Ask and Ye Shall Save

Not long ago, I tore my patellar tendon falling on top of Masada in Israel (an ancient fortress—long story). I waited until I was back in the US for surgery, partly because I quickly discovered Israeli hospitals don't believe in pain meds—and I *do*.

A few months into recovery, I got a call saying I owed $1,500 to the surgical center. I hadn't seen a bill yet, but I asked, "If I paid today, could you offer a discount?"

Without hesitation: "Sure—25% off if you pay by card right now."
Done.

Since then, I've learned that hospitals, doctors, and outpatient clinics often offer 25–40% discounts for lump-sum payments or if you're paying without insurance.

Cable and Streaming Services: Loyalty Has Leverage

Before I cut the cord, I used to visit my cable provider every year when the price went up. With a smile and a little story about being a long-time customer, I almost always walked out at a reduced rate.

Now, with streaming or satellite radio, the trick is the same: Call, mention you're thinking of canceling, and ask if they have any current promos. Chances are, they do.

I routinely get 50% off my SiriusXM subscription just by asking.

Insurance Premiums: Discounts You Didn't Know You Could Ask For

Most insurance policies (home, auto, umbrella) creep up over time, even without claims. What many people don't know is that insurance underwriters can apply "credits" or discounts of 10–30% if prompted.

Call your agent and say:

> "I don't want to shop around, but I'll have to unless we can find some ways to lower the premium."

Also, shop for insurance every 2–3 years. New customers often get better deals than loyal ones.

Cell Phone Bills: The Hidden Discounts

I've spent way too much time on the phone with cellular companies, but I've also saved hundreds. The key? Ask if there's a new plan, a loyalty discount, or if they can waive a recent fee.

Be patient, be polite, and don't be afraid to escalate politely to a supervisor. Persistence pays.

Auto Purchases: Negotiate or Overpay—There's No In-Between

This one's a given: never pay sticker price for a car. Whether you're buying new or used, there's always room for negotiation on the sale price, the trade-in value, and the extras.

Check out Baker's Principle #7 for the full breakdown on car-buying strategy.

Hotels: Ask and Save (Even Last Minute)

Even if you're an Airbnb regular, hotel rooms can still be a great deal—if you ask.

1. Look up the best rate on travel sites.
2. Call the hotel directly and say, "I found this online for $X. Can you beat it if I book directly?"

I've also walked right into hotel lobbies, pulled up their room rates on travel apps, and politely asked if they could beat the price. Guess what? They have every time. In fact, I recently did this and saved about 50% on a night's stay just for asking.

Hotels often prefer direct bookings (no commission to pay the site) and may offer better rates, upgrades, or perks. Also ask about:

- AAA discounts
- Government or military rates
- Medical stay discounts (They saved me $60 at a Texas hotel! That one trick saved me $60 a night at a Texas hotel near the hospital, proving once again that bedside manner is important.)

College Tuition: More Negotiable Than You Think

Did you know that most students do not pay the full sticker price? In 2019–2020, only 26% of in-state public college students and only 16% of students enrolled in private, nonprofit institutions paid the sticker price.[17]

When one of my daughters was applying to college, we learned that her college of choice offered department-specific scholarships. She was a Spanish major, so I encouraged her to meet the Humanities Department head during her campus visit.

Later, she applied for the Presidential Scholarship through that department and won it.

Maybe she would've earned it anyway. But when the decision-makers know your name and story? It doesn't hurt.

> "It's not the grades you make—
> it's the hands you shake."
>
> **John Bradley, former student**

Other Things You Can—and Should—Negotiate

- **Rent:** Especially when renewing a lease. Timing, market conditions, and being a good tenant can work in your favor.
- **Real Estate Commissions:** The standard 6% isn't set in stone. Many agents will reduce their fee by 0.5–1% to win your listing.

---

17. Phillip Levine, "Ignore the sticker price: How have college prices really changes?" *Brookings*, April 12, 2024, https://www.brookings.edu/articles/ignore-the-sticker-price-how-have-college-prices-really-changed.

- **Hotel Room add-ons:** Parking, late check-out, or breakfast—these can often be comped or discounted.
- **College Work-Study and Grants:** Build relationships with the financial aid office. Ask early and often.
- **IRS Payment Plans:** If you owe taxes, the IRS will work with you on an installment plan. Better to ask than to ignore it.

> **BAKER'S HINT:** Want to save some cash? Try paying with cash. It sounds old school, but it works, especially with service pros like plumbers, electricians, or HVAC folks. I recently had a new roof put on my farmhouse (thanks, wear and tear), and I asked the contractor, "What kind of discount do I get if I pay you in cold, hard cash?" He didn't even blink and promptly knocked 10% off the price. Apparently, Benjamins talk louder than checks.

Final Word: Don't Be Afraid to Ask

Negotiation isn't about being pushy.

It's about being informed and intentional.

The key? Ask politely. Know your options. And always be ready to walk away or smile and say thank you if the answer's no.

More often than not, you'll be surprised at how many people are willing to work with you.

And the best part? Every dollar you don't spend is a dollar you keep.

BILL DAILEY: Wait—Free HDTV Is Still a Thing?

Yep, you read that right. In the age of streaming, subscriptions, and endless monthly fees, it's easy to forget you can still get live, high-definition TV totally free. No cable, no internet—just an antenna and a TV.

After the big switch from analog to digital back in 2009, a lot of people thought over-the-air TV was gone for good. Spoiler: it's not. You just need a digital antenna (they're cheap online) and a TV that can scan for local channels.

Setup is easy: plug in the antenna, follow your TV's scan instructions, and boom—you've got live HDTV from major networks, all for zero dollars.

Pros? It's free and HD. Cons? Fewer channels and maybe some drama with your HOA if they're not fans of visible antennas. But don't worry . . .

Thanks to a little something called the Over-the-Air Reception Devices rule (yeah, it's a mouthful), you're legally protected. Written to enforce a part of the Telecommunications Act of 1996, this rule bans "restrictions that impair the installation, maintenance or use of antennas used to receive video pro-gramming." It even covers renters, so if you've got a balcony, patio, or personal slice of outdoor space, you're good to go.

Baker's Dirty Dozen
PRINCIPLE #6
Break Free from the Chains of Debt

SHANE LESTER: From Get-Rich-Quick to Actually Getting Ahead

I got sucked into the get-rich-quick trap. I tried everything: Forex trading (where I lost $60,000 overnight), options trading, tax liens, stock tips—you name it. We even managed to lose our entire retirement three separate times. If there's a shortcut to wealth, trust me, I took it . . . and paid the price.

For the average American, there is no secret formula for building wealth quickly. That's a hard truth I had to learn the hard way.

One Sunday, walking out of church, I spotted a copy of *The Total Money Makeover* by Dave Ramsey. I've always been drawn to books about money, so I downloaded the audiobook. From the first chapter, I was hooked. It just made sense.

Two questions hit me like a ton of bricks:

1. What could you do if you didn't owe anybody any money?
2. How much money have you and your wife made over the last eight years?

I had never considered either question—and I didn't like the answers. My wife and I were two working professionals with a combined income, yet we'd blown through an embarrassing amount of money. At that point, it had been six years since we filed for bankruptcy . . . and we were still $250,000 in debt.

That book changed everything.

We made drastic changes at home: paid off student loans, used cash envelopes to stay on budget, and committed to living below our means.

It wasn't glamorous, and it wasn't fast—but within a few years, we were completely debt-free.

Best of all, we've now been able to give generously in ways we never imagined possible. No gimmicks. Just discipline, humility, and a whole lot of budgeting envelopes.

You'll often hear this in financial circles: "There's good debt and there's bad debt."

"Good debt" is usually defined as anything tied to an appreciating asset, like a mortgage or student loan. "Bad debt" is your usual suspects: credit cards, payday loans, and other high-interest villains lurking in your wallet.

But here's my take, shaped by decades of experience and the peace that came with ditching the debt: All debt is bad.

Some of it might be necessary, especially when you're starting out and building a life. But necessary doesn't mean good—it just means you're trying to get from point A to point B without falling completely flat.

Buying a home, getting a degree, or even snagging your first (reliable-ish) car might require debt. Fine. But let's be clear: that should be the exception, not the strategy.

I've heard folks, some smart, some related to me, say things like, "You'll always have a mortgage" or "Car loans are just part of life."

Nope. I respectfully and wholeheartedly disagree.

The moment I became completely debt-free was the moment I felt real financial freedom. No payments due. No interest quietly nibbling at my future. Just peace . . . and the quiet satisfaction of knowing the only thing I owed was a thank-you to my past self.

JUSTIN MORRELLA: Lessons from a 2 a.m. Repo

Like many young entrepreneurs, I launched my business with more confidence than preparation. In 2017, I quit my full-time job, bought a shiny new truck, and started a handyman business with no savings, no business plan, and plenty of blind optimism. I thought, *If I can make decent money on the side, why not go all in and scale it tenfold?*

It wasn't that easy.

I knew construction, but I didn't know business. Within two years, I had a small crew on payroll and was doing everything I could to keep them paid, even if it meant falling behind on my own bills. I learned quickly, and painfully, that passion alone doesn't pay invoices.

Then came the literal wake-up call at 2 a.m. My phone lit up with texts, and I could hear the tow truck outside. I didn't even get up. I knew what was happening: I was three payments behind, and the truck I'd once been so proud of was being repossessed. My neighbor knocked to let me know, but I couldn't bring myself to answer the door. I was embarrassed, overwhelmed, and completely unprepared.

For the next year, I drove a beat-up car. But it ran, and more importantly, it gave me space to reflect. After five years of financial strain, my wife and I sat down, made a plan, and committed to budgeting and rebuilding. In 2022, I cut the payroll, picked up my own toolbelt again, and focused on reducing debt and increasing profit.

Today, we co-own a seven-figure construction company. My wife now works alongside me full time, and she challenges me every day to be better. I'm proud of the business we've built, but I'm even more proud that I didn't quit when things got tough.

THE DEBT DIVIDE:
WHAT THE NUMBERS TELL US

Debt doesn't discriminate. Every generation deals with it, but the kind and amount vary drastically. Here's how the burden breaks down today:

Gen Z (1997-2012)

Gen Z is the first generation to grow up entirely in the digital era, giving them a unique edge in navigating modern finance, yet they're also entering adulthood during a time of rising debt, economic uncertainty, and shifting career norms.

- This generation is more focused, financially aware, and investing in their future with a mix of caution and ambition compared to previous generations.[1]
- They make up 28.2% of student loan borrowers, and as more enter college, their debt load is growing fast. With many aiming to be the most educated generation, borrowing is expected to climb.[2]

Millennials (1981-1996)

Millennials have been hit hardest. They're earning less (adjusted for inflation) and starting adult life with more debt than any previous generation.

- Nearly one-third of Millennials carry student loan debt.
- They have faced a brutal housing market, being priced out by rising costs, low inventory, and years of stagnant wages just as they reached peak home-buying age.[3] They have the highest mortgage debt of any generation.[4]
- Over 60% say their debt is delaying major life decisions like home buying, marriage, or starting a family.[5]

It's no surprise that this group also reports the lowest level of financial confidence when it comes to both short- and long-term decisions.

Generation X (1965-1980)

Often overshadowed by the buzz around millennials and Gen Z, Gen X is quietly carrying some of the heaviest financial burdens. Caught between aging parents and grown children, they're navigating one of the most expensive phases of life.

1. Caitlin Nuttall, "12 Characteristics of Gen Z in 2025," *GWI*, August 5, 2025, https://www.gwi.com/blog/generation-z-characteristics.
2. Melanie Hanson, "Student Loan Debt by Generation," *Education Data Initiative*, November 21, 2024, https://educationdata.org/student-loan-debt-by-generation.
3. Mike Winters and Gabriel Cortés, "28-year-old made 15 offers, went $65,000 over asking price and still got rejected: The housing market is 'a slap in the face,'" *CNBC Make It*, September 18, 2024, https://www.cnbc.com/2024/09/17/frustrated-millennials-across-the-us-struggle-to-afford-homes.html.
4. Brad Tuttle, "Which Generation Has the Most Debt? It's Not Millennials," *Money*, June 4, 2024, https://money.com/generation-with-most-debt-gen-x/.
5. "Report 72% of Non-Homeowners with Student Debt Believe Loans Will Delay Home Purchase," *Fairway Home Mortgage*, October 5, 2021, https://www.fairway.com/articles/student-debt-delays-home-purchase.

- They carry the highest average debt of any generation at $157,556, driven by mortgages, education costs, and ongoing family support.[6]
- With retirement still on the horizon, they're juggling college tuition, healthcare costs, and daily living expenses all at once.
- Despite being in their peak earning years, Gen X often feels financially squeezed—and is frequently left out of broader generational financial narratives.
- They also have the highest average credit card debt of all generations.[7]

Baby Boomers (1946-1964)

Boomers are often viewed as the most financially secure generation, however there are some warning signs for this group:

- In a recent survey conduction by the National Debt Relief, nearly half of the survey respondents said they have only $20k or less in savings.
- In the same survey, nearly 50% reported having credit card debt with a balance of nearly $9,000.[8]
- Nearly 1 in 4 Boomers have borrowed from their retirement savings at some point.[9]

Pulling from retirement too early can have a snowball effect, especially when combined with rising healthcare costs and longer lifespans.

6. Brad Tuttle, "Which Generation Has the Most Debt? It's Not Millennials," *Money*, June 4, 2024, https://money.com/generation-with-most-debt-gen-x/.

7. Ibid.

8. Renee Oehlerking, "Debt Is a Reality for Most Older Americans, Putting Retirement Plans on Hold," *National Debt Relief*, April 2025, https://www.nationaldebtrelief.com/news-media/debt-is-a-reality-for-most-older-americans-putting-retirement-plans-on-hold/.

9. Kaili Killpack, "Survey Finds 1 in 4 Boomers Have No Savings, Why Americans Are Afraid They Can't Make Ends Meet In Retirement," *Yahoo Finance*, June 12, 2024, https://finance.yahoo.com/news/survey-finds-1-4-boomers-154513768.html.

LET'S RETHINK WHAT'S "NORMAL"

Debt has been normalized. It's marketed to us as a tool, a strategy, even a lifestyle. But here's the truth:

Debt is not a wealth-building tool.
It's a wealth-draining anchor.

You may need it at some points in life, but don't get comfortable with it. Don't build your budget around it. Don't believe the myth that you'll "always" have it.

What if, instead of accepting debt as inevitable, you started treating it like the obstacle it is? What if you made eliminating it a priority, not just a someday goal?

Because real freedom doesn't come when you make more money. It comes when you don't owe any of it to anyone else.

> **BAKER'S REMINDER:** "If you want to build wealth, you've got to stop sending pieces of your paycheck to banks, credit card companies, and lenders every month."

MATTHEW NELSON: Cold Air, Warm Wallet:
How Alaska Helped Melt My Student Debt

Before I even graduated pharmacy school, debt was already breathing down my neck. I'd been debt-free once before, and I knew what I was giving up: freedom. I realized something big: Debt is like modern-day indentured servitude. So I decided to do something about it. I cooked nearly every meal at home, learned to do my own car maintenance, and drove a 1995 Nissan Altima with 340,000 miles. It still had cold A/C, working heat, and great gas mileage. My parents had given it to me after putting 100,000 miles on it themselves, telling me, "Just leave it on the side of the road if it blows up. We got our money's worth."

But frugality alone wasn't going to wipe out six figures of student loans. I needed to earn more—a lot more. So, I started looking into places that offered both higher pay and tax advantages. Alaska checked every box: no income tax, no sales tax, and 25–40% higher pay due to the remoteness. Sure, the cost of living was higher, but the math still came out way ahead. When a strong offer and generous benefits package arrived, it was a no-brainer.

Fast forward to now: I've been working in one of the most beautiful places on earth for over a year. In just 12 months, I've paid off $59,000, nearly 30% of my student loan debt. With 85% of my income going to debt, rent, bills, and food, I've managed to stay focused while still enjoying life and making progress. At this pace, I'll be debt-free in five years, possibly four, if I tighten things up even more.

The "Alaska strategy" is working. Financial freedom isn't just a dream; it's in sight.

DEBT'S SNEAKY COUSIN: CREDIT

Debt shows up like a wrecking ball. But credit is more subtle. It shows up in a suit, offers you points and perks, and then quietly charges you 26% interest. Let's take a closer look at credit before it takes a closer look at your wallet.

To understand debt, you have to understand credit—what it is, how it works, and how it can either be a useful tool or a dangerous trap.

A good credit score has become a sort of modern currency.

You need it to:

- Rent an apartment
- Get approved for a mortgage
- Qualify for business loans
- Secure a decent auto or homeowners insurance rate

But here's the part that rarely gets talked about: A high credit score doesn't necessarily mean you're good with money. Often, it just means you're good at borrowing and repaying large sums of money.

If that sounds backward to you, you're not alone. According to Baker's Dirty Dozen Principles, borrowing large sums of money isn't something to be rewarded, but rather something to be avoided. If you use a credit card, the only acceptable method is to pay it off in full every single month. Do that, and you'll build a healthy credit score without debt becoming your lifestyle.

So What *Is* Credit, Really?

Think of credit as financial trust with a price tag. It allows you to get something now like money, goods, or services with the promise to repay it later, usually with interest.

> **Credit:** "A contractual agreement in which a borrower receives something of value now and agrees to repay the lender at a later date—generally with interest."[10]

> Simple in theory. Powerful and sometimes painful in practice.

What Can Bad Credit Really Cost You?

Having poor credit (or no credit at all) can impact more than just loan applications. It can affect your job prospects, living situation, monthly expenses, and insurance premiums. Here's how:

1. You Could Be Denied a Job.

Yes—your credit could cost you a job.

More employers, especially those hiring for roles that involve money, sensitive data, or security, are including credit checks as part of the application process. According to a Demos study, about 1 in 4 job applicants reported that a potential employer ran a credit check. Poor credit may be seen (fairly or unfairly) as a sign of irresponsibility.[11]

2. It Affects Your Mortgage and Refinance Rates.

Your credit score is one of the most important factors in determining your mortgage rate. A low score could mean paying tens of thousands more in interest over the life of your loan.

Want to refinance later? That score still matters.

(See more on this in Baker's Principle #10.)

---

10. "Credit: What It Is and How It Works," *Investopedia*, October 1, 2024, https://www.investopedia.com/terms/c/credit.asp.

11. Amy Traub, "Discredited: How Employment Credit Checks Keep Qualified Workers Out of a Job," *Dēmos*, February 3, 2014, https://www.demos.org/research/discredited-how-employment-credit-checks-keep-qualified-workers-out-job.

3. It Can Keep You from Renting a Home.

Landlords routinely run credit checks. They're trying to answer one question: "Will this person pay on time?" If your report shows late payments, collections, or high debt loads, you could be denied or asked to pay a larger deposit.

4. It Impacts Your Auto and Home Insurance Rates.

Having worked in the insurance world for years, I can confirm: your credit score is baked into your premium. According to research by Conning & Co., 92% of insurance companies use credit history when underwriting new policies.[12] Even if you've never made a claim, poor credit could mean a higher rate.

5. When It Comes to Borrowing for College, Not All Student Loans Play by the Same Rules.

Your credit score doesn't impact the interest rate on federal student loans because everyone gets the same deal there. But with private student loans, your credit score can be the difference between a manageable single-digit rate and a painful double-digit one. Lenders use a few different credit scoring models, but most of them rely on your FICO score when reviewing your application.[13]

6. It Increases Your Car Loan Interest Rate.

Car loan lenders often structure their deals around your credit score. The lower your score, the higher your rate and the more you'll pay over time. My hope? You reach a place where you never need a car loan again. (See Baker's Principle #7.)

Credit Score Breakdown (Just So You Know)

A "good" interest rate can vary depending on your credit and overall financial picture. But here's a general breakdown of what qualifies as a good rate based on your credit score:

---

12. GEICO, *GEICO's Credit Use – Frequently Asked Questions*, citing Conning & Co., accessed September 4, 2025, https://www.geico.com/information/credit-use-faq.
13. Denny Ceizyk, "What credit score is needed for a student loan?" *Bankrate*, April 14, 2025, https://www.bankrate.com/loans/student-loans/credit-score-for-student-loans.

Credit Standing	Credit Score	Good Interest Rate
Excellent	750+	3% to 4%
Good	700–749	4% to 5%
Fair	650–699	6% to 8%
Poor	600–649	9% to 12%

My hope is that you will reach a place where you never need a car loan again. (See Baker's Principle #7 on buying vehicles with cash.)

> **BAKER'S TIP:** You can check your credit score for free with services like Credit Karma or NerdWallet or through your bank or credit card provider. Also, bank apps are now showing credit scores and a link to check out credit history.

Baker's Bottom Line on Credit

A good credit score is just a tool. It's not a sign of wealth but rather a sign of behavior. Use it wisely, and never let it lead you into a lifestyle you can't afford.

If you're using credit to build a life you can't pay for, you're not building at all—you're borrowing from your future. Let's flip that script. Use credit as a bridge, not a crutch.

How to Improve Your Credit—Without Going into Debt

You don't have to carry a balance or rack up debt to build a strong credit score. Here are Baker-approved ways to improve (and maintain) your credit the smart way:

1. Always Pay On Time.

Payment history makes up 35% of your credit score. Even one missed payment can ding your score significantly. Set up auto-pay or reminders so you never forget.

2. Use a Credit Card—But Pay It Off Monthly.

Make small purchases you'd make anyway (groceries, gas, phone bill), then pay the balance in full each month. This shows lenders you're responsible *without* racking up interest.

3. Keep Your Credit Utilization Low.

Use less than 30% of your total credit limit (ideally less than 10%). If your card limit is $5,000, try to keep your balance under $500 at any given time.

4. Check Your Credit Reports Annually.

Get free reports from all three bureaus (Equifax, Experian, TransUnion) at AnnualCreditReport.com. Look for errors or fraud—and dispute anything that doesn't belong.

> **BAKER'S BONUS TIP:** Don't apply for too much credit at once. Each application creates a "hard inquiry," which can temporarily lower your score. Space out new credit applications and only apply when needed.

"You don't have to borrow money to build good credit; you just have to be intentional."

Real-Life Example: Car Loan Rates

Look at this recreation of a Truth-In-Lending Disclosure statement below from an actual car buyer.[14]

New/Used	Year	Make and Model	Vehicle Identification Number
NEW	2019	VOLKSWA TIGUAN	XXXXXXXXXXXXXXX

---

14. Courtesy of Shane T. Lester, CMC®, CRMP®, CRMS®, owner of Wonder State Mortgage and Reverse Mortgages of Arkansas. Obtained in 2020.

FEDERAL TRUTH-IN-LENDING DISCLOSURES				
ANNUAL PERCENTAGE RATE The cost of your credit as a yearly rate.	**FINANCE CHARGE** The dollar amount the credit will cost you.	**AMOUNT FINANCED** The amount of credit provided to you or on your behalf.	**TOTAL OF PAYMENTS** The amount you will have paid after you have made all payments as scheduled.	**TOTAL SALE PRICE** The total cost of your purchase on credit, including your down payment of $ 0.00 is
21.50%	$ 33,057.13	$ 41,138.15	$ 74,195.28	$ 74,195.28
Your Payment Schedule Will Be:				
Number of Payments	**Amount of Payments**	**When Payments Are Due**		
72	$ 1,030.49	Monthly beginning AUGUST 25, 2019		

Notice the sale price is $41,138. Now let's review the rest of the information and assess the true cost:

- 21.5% interest rate (Yikes! I would assume a terrible credit score.)
- Total finance charges: $33,057
- Number of payments: 72 months (6 years)
- Total cost of the vehicle: $74,195

I'm not saying you shouldn't buy a nice vehicle, but there's a time and place for every car-buying decision. It's important to understand the opportunity cost involved. Spending a significant amount on a car is a major financial decision, and often, the long-term impact is underestimated.

The person making that purchase may not be making a reckless choice; they may simply lack the financial education to see the full picture. But regardless of intent, they'll still have to face the financial consequences.

That's where Baker's Dirty Dozen Principles come in, offering a smarter framework to help you make intentional, informed choices when it comes to buying a vehicle.

Credit Scores and FICO® Scores: What's the Difference?

Understanding how credit works is essential to understanding debt. One key part of your credit profile is your *credit score*. This is a three-digit number that reflects how likely you are to repay borrowed money. But not all credit scores are created equal, and not all are used the same way.

Credit Score vs. FICO® Score

Let's break it down.

Credit scores are used by lenders, like banks and credit card companies, to evaluate your creditworthiness. They typically range from 300 to 850, and yes, you may have several different scores, depending on which credit bureau or scoring model is used.

One of the most widely used types of credit scores is the FICO® Score, created by the Fair Isaac Corporation. While "credit score" is a general term, FICO® is a specific brand and the one most commonly used for major lending decisions, especially mortgages.[15]

> **BAKER'S BOTTOM LINE:** All FICO® scores are credit scores, but not all credit scores are FICO® scores.

Baker's Picks: Where to Check Your Score

Credit Karma and **Credit Sesame** offer free credit scores, but *not* FICO® scores. These are helpful tools for monitoring trends and changes.

> **BAKER'S CHOICE:** You can get a *free FICO® score* from Discover, even if you're not a customer.[16]

---

15. "What is a Credit Score?" *MyFICO*, accessed September 4, 2025, https://www.myfico.com/credit-education/credit-scores.
16. See https://www.discover.com/credit-cards/free-credit-score/.

What's in a FICO® Score?

FICO® Scores are calculated using five categories, each with a different weight:[17]

Category	Weight	What It Means
Payment History	35%	Are you paying your bills on time? Late payments hurt you most.
Amounts Owed	30%	How much of your available credit are you using?
Length of Credit History	15%	How long have your accounts been open? Longer is better.
Credit Mix	10%	Do you have a healthy mix (credit cards, loans, mortgage)?
New Credit	10%	How many accounts have you opened recently? Too many = red flag.

What's a *Good* FICO® Score?

According to FICO®:[18]

- **800+** = Exceptional
- **740–799** = Very Good
- **670–739** = Good (and near the US average)
- **580–669** = Fair
- **Below 580** = Poor

How to Get Your Full Credit Report (Not Just the Score)

Every year, you're entitled to one free credit report from each of the three major credit bureaus:

- TransUnion
- Equifax
- Experian

Get yours at AnnualCreditReport.com—the only government-backed site authorized for free reports.

---

17. *"How Are FICO Scores Calculated?" MyFICO,* last updated October 1, 2024, https://www.myfico.com/credit-education/whats-in-your-credit-score.
18. "What Is a FICO Score and Why Is It Important?" *MyFICO,* last updated October 1, 2024, https://www.myfico.com/credit-education/whats-in-your-credit-score.

These reports show your credit history, but not your credit score.

Why Should You Check Your Credit Report?

- Spot errors or fraudulent activity
- Catch signs of identity theft early
- Understand what lenders (or employers) may see
- Take control of your financial health

Even one mistake, like a payment wrongly reported as late, can hurt your score. Stay informed.

Just Starting Out? How to Build Credit Without Debt

If you're just beginning your credit journey, you may feel stuck in the classic Credit Catch-22: *"I need credit to build credit, but no one will give me credit because I don't have credit."*

Here are a few ways to get started:

1. Apply for a Secured Credit Card.

- You make a refundable cash deposit (say, $300).
- That amount becomes your credit limit.
- Use the card *responsibly*, paying off balances in full.
- Over time, you build a score and may graduate to an unsecured card.

Browse secured card options at Credit Karma–Secured Cards.[19]

2. Use a Store Credit Card Carefully.

Store cards often have lower credit requirements, but higher interest rates. If used sparingly and paid off monthly, they can help build a credit history.

3. Become an Authorized User.

A trusted family member or friend can add you as an authorized user on their credit card. You benefit from their good history *without being responsible for the debt* (just don't abuse their trust).

---

19. See https://www.creditkarma.com/credit-cards/secured-credit-cards.

The goal is not to chase a perfect score. The goal is to build healthy financial habits that lead to freedom and not more borrowing.

CREDIT CARDS: CONVENIENCE OR TRAP?

"If you cannot pay the balance off in full every month, you cannot afford it."

Baker's Rule of Credit Cards

Credit card debt is one of the fastest ways to derail your financial goals. It often starts small—thanks to minimum payment options, promotional 0% interest offers, and flashy rewards programs. But without discipline, it can quickly grow into a financial monster.

With average interest rates ranging from 10–30% APR, credit card balances can snowball into long-term debt traps that feel nearly impossible to escape.

APR (Annual Percentage Rate) is the yearly cost of borrowing, including interest and fees.[20]

KATIE MATSON: Broke, Buried, and Rebuilt

I grew up poor in a small town where money struggles were public and shameful. My dad only bought what he could afford, and while we knew our limits, we never talked about money, especially not how to manage it.

At 18, I got my first credit card and felt financial freedom for the first time. I quickly maxed it out and had no idea how badly it could affect my future. By my mid-20s, I was drowning in credit card debt and collections, with no real plan.

When my beat-up car finally died, I couldn't get a loan and had to ask my dad to co-sign. It was humiliating. That moment pushed me to take control. I pulled my credit report, tackled collections, and started budgeting. I relearned the lesson from childhood: if I couldn't afford it outright, I wouldn't buy it.

---

20. Jason Fernando, "Annual Percentage Rate (APR): Definition, Calculation, and Comparison," *Investopedia*, August 13, 2025, https://www.investopedia.com/terms/a/apr.asp.

At 30, I drained my savings to move across the country and start over. I took my real estate career seriously, built a $50,000 savings cushion, opened a 401(k), and raised my credit score from the low 600s to 790.

My biggest shift? Learning to live below my means, even as my income grew. That financial stability gave me freedom to travel, pursue photography, and spend on experiences with people I love.

Financial literacy is hard, especially if you start behind. But the moment you stop surviving and start building, everything begins to change.

Step One: Organize Your Debt

Start by listing all your current debts such as credit cards, auto loans, personal loans, student loans. Then sort them by:

1. Interest Rate (highest to lowest)
2. Outstanding Balance (lowest to highest)

This gives you a clear picture of what you're working with and helps determine your payoff strategy.

Two Popular Payoff Methods: Snowball vs. Avalanche

You've probably heard of these two approaches to becoming debt-free. Both are effective, but the best one depends on your mindset and motivation.

The Snowball Method
Start small. Build momentum. Get quick wins.

The snowball method focuses on paying off your smallest balances first, while making minimum payments on all other debts. As each small debt is paid off, you roll the freed-up payment amount into the next smallest balance, like a snowball gaining size and speed.

Pros
- ✓ Boosts confidence early
- ✓ Reduces the number of accounts faster
- ✓ Feels motivating

Debt Type	Balance	Rate	Min. Payment
Personal Loan	$2,000	7%	$39.60
Student Loan	$13,000	5%	$183.74
Credit Card	$16,000	17%	$480.00
Auto Loan	$21,559	4.75%	$404.38

Let's say you have $100/month extra to pay toward debt:

- Pay $139.60 toward your personal loan (minimum + $100).
- After it's gone, roll that $139.60 toward the student loan.
- Repeat the process until you're debt-free.[21]

The Avalanche Method
Target the interest. Save more in the long run.

The avalanche method has you pay off the debt with the highest interest rate first, while still making minimum payments on all other debts.

In the above example, you would:

- Put the $100 toward the credit card (17% APR).
- Once paid off, move to the personal loan (7% APR).
- Continue down the list.

Pros
- ✓ Minimizes total interest paid
- ✓ May pay off debt faster overall

---

21. Justin Pritchard, "What Is the Debt Snowball Strategy?" *The Balance*, January 5, 2023, https://www.thebalance .com/what-is-debt-snowball-1293674.

Snowball or Avalanche—Which Is Best?

There's no universal answer. The snowball method helps you see progress quickly, which can be motivating. The avalanche method is more mathematically efficient.

> **BAKER'S TAKE?** Choose the method that works *for your personality.* Just don't ignore the debt.

Baker's Choice: Helpful Apps

There are several mobile apps to help you stay on track using either method:

- Debt Free
- Debt Payoff Pro
- Debt Manager
- Debt Strategy

Most of these let you plug in your debts, pick a method, and follow a visual progress tracker.

What About Balance Transfers?

A credit card balance transfer involves moving your balance from a high-interest card to one with a lower rate, sometimes even 0% for a limited time.

Potential Benefits

- ✓ Lower interest
- ✓ Faster payoff

Watch Out For

- ✗ Balance transfer fees (usually 3–5%)
- ✗ The expiration of the 0% APR promo (which may jump to 20%+)
- ✗ A good credit score is typically required to qualify

> **BAKER'S TIP:** Do your homework before signing up. A balance transfer without a plan can turn into another trap.

Real-Life Example: The Cost of the Minimum Payment

Let's say you have a $4,854 balance on a credit card with a 19.49% APR. The minimum payment is $165/month.

Seems doable, right? Not so fast.

If you only pay the minimum each month:

- It will take you 26 years to pay it off.
- You'll pay over $10,097 in total (more than double your original balance).
- That's with zero new purchases, which almost never happens.

Minimum payments aren't mercy; they're a trap.

A survey by the Consumer Financial Protection Bureau found that nearly half of all credit card holders pay off their balance each month. That means the other half are carrying balances and often paying steep interest rates to do so.[22]

STUDENT LOANS

Yes, you have to pay them off (and can!)

If you do not have any student loans (or only a small amount), you can skip this section. However, I would encourage you to call your parents, grandparents, or whoever helped you financially and tell them thanks for helping you get a head start toward your financial independence.

=== **DR. LEVI ELLISON, PHARMD:** From Six Figures to Freedom: ===
How We Crushed $214k in 17 Months

When my wife and I graduated from pharmacy school in May 2018, we were thrilled to be earning a combined $265,000 a year. But with that income came baggage, specifically, $208,000 in student loans. And thanks to interest, that number was growing by more than $1,000 a month.

---

22. Paul Soucy, "Credit Card Data, Statistics and Research," *Nerdwallet*, September 1, 2025, https://www.nerd wallet.com/article/credit-cards/credit-card-data. See also Consumer Financial Protection Bureau, *The Consumer Credit Card Market Report*, October 2023, https://files.consumerfinance.gov/f/documents/cfpb _consumer-credit-card-market-report_2023.pdf.

Why the urgency to pay it off? Simple, because we wanted to live and give like no one else. We didn't want debt dictating our decisions. A free copy of *The Total Money Makeover* in Mr. Baker's class gave us the roadmap, and we followed it like our lives depended on it. We paid off $214,594.55 in just 17 months, about $400 a day, and celebrated becoming debt-free in December 2019.

How did we do it? With discipline, sacrifice, and one word on repeat: *budget*. We made a plan before every month began, paid off debts smallest to largest, and ate at home religiously. We still tithed, gave gifts, and celebrated milestones, but all within the boundaries of our budget. Our life wasn't joyless; it was just intentionally lived.

Today, we don't work to pay off the past; we work to invest in our future and give generously. Financial emergencies are now just mild inconveniences. Want true freedom? Pay the price. And if you miss the debt lifestyle . . . don't worry, it's always waiting for you.

The Student Loan Crisis: A Crisis of Cost and Confidence

There's little doubt you're already aware of the student loan crisis in the United States. You might even be living it. And if you're not, someone close to you probably is.

The numbers alone are staggering:

- Total student loan debt: Over $1.78 trillion and rising[23]
- Average federal student loan debt balance is $38,375, while the total average balance (including private loan debt) may be as high as $41,618.
- Average graduate student debt: Approximately $88,220[24]
- College tuition has increased by 710% between 1983–2023, while the Consumer Price Index (CPI) has risen by only 194% over the same period.[25]

23. Melanie Hanson, "Student Loan Debt Statistics," *Education Data Initiative*, August 8, 2025, https://education data.org/student-loan-debt-statistics.
24. Melanie Hanson, "Average Student Loan Debt," *Education Data Initiative*, September 1, 2024, https://education data.org/average-graduate-student-loan-debt.
25. Reddit user u/Marky_Mark, "College Tuition Has Increased a Whole Lot Faster Than Wages," *Reddit*, April 23, 2021, https://www.reddit.com/r/dataisbeautiful/comments/mzpyau/college_tuition_has_increased_a _whole_lot_faster/.

But perhaps the most sobering statistic is this: Nearly half of indebted millennials think college wasn't worth taking out student loans, according to an *Insider* and *Morning Consult* survey.[26]

Let that sink in.

This crisis isn't just about money; it's about trust. Confidence in the system is eroding. Today's borrowers aren't just struggling to repay loans—they're struggling to navigate a chaotic, ever-changing system with moving goalposts.

As of early 2025, more than 4 million borrowers have been marked delinquent, and projections suggest that number could climb to 9 million, which is a potentially record-breaking wave of defaults. These aren't all people avoiding payment. Many are trying to pay but are caught in a dysfunctional system overwhelmed by backlogs, confusion, and contradictory instructions.

After nearly five years of paused payments due to the pandemic, the federal government has now fully resumed collections. But the restart has been far from smooth. An overwhelmed Department of Education, legal disputes over new repayment plans, and under-resourced loan servicers have left borrowers in the dark. Many report receiving bills double what they expected, spending hours on hold, and receiving no clear answers. Meanwhile, more than a million borrowers are stuck in limbo waiting on the processing of income-driven repayment plans.

And this isn't new. The roots of the student loan system stretch back decades, from the Cold War-inspired National Defense Education Act of 1958 to the Higher Education Act of 1965, to major overhauls in 2010 when the government took full control of the federal lending system. What began as a modest program to expand opportunity has ballooned into a multi-trillion-dollar industry, plagued by unintended consequences and little reform.

Today, the system is unpredictable, politically charged, and largely unprepared to serve the 38 million borrowers now expected to repay. It's no surprise that trust is fading, and the stakes are enormous. Credit damage, delayed milestones, and financial stress are just the beginning. A broken

---

26. Hillary Hoffower, "Nearly half of indebted millennials say college wasn't worth it, and the reason why is obvious," *Business Insider*, April 11, 2019, https://www.businessinsider.com/personal-finance/millennials-college-not-worth-student-loan-debt-2019-4.

repayment system doesn't just hurt individuals, it casts a shadow over the economy and the promise of higher education itself.[27]

What This Means for You

Whether you're planning for college, currently enrolled, or already in repayment, one thing is clear: student loans are no longer just a financial decision. They're a risk-management challenge.

So Now What? Where Are the Solutions?

"Blah, blah, blah—I get it. Student loan debt is bad. So what can I *do* about it?"

I hear you. You can't rely on the system to work in your favor, or even work reliably at all. And while we can't fix the entire student loan infrastructure here, this chapter is about equipping you with the tools, mindset, and strategies to navigate it, regardless of how broken it may be.

Pre-College: Education Before Debt

High school seniors should not be entering adulthood without understanding how student loans work, or without being aware of all their post-secondary options. A required semester-long course in financial literacy could be transformational. Topics should include:

- How student loans work (interest, deferment, repayment)
- How to fill out FAFSA
- How to apply for scholarships and grants
- Basics of budgeting and financial responsibility
- Career pathways, income potential, and job market demand
- Trade school and skilled career alternatives

Most students don't know that electricians, plumbers, welders, and other skilled trade workers often earn more than many four-year college grads, without the debt burden. Education should empower students to choose *what's right for them*, not just what culture suggests.

---

27. *The Daily*, "Is the Era of Student Loan Forgiveness Officially Over?" hosted by Sabrina Tavernise, featuring Stacy Cowley, *The New York Times*, April 21, 2025, https://www.iheart.com/podcast/326-the-daily-28076606 /episode/is-the-era-of-student-loan-273027615.

During College: Awareness Before Acceptance

Higher education institutions share responsibility for the student loan crisis. Loan offices should require students to attend interactive loan education seminars before funds are disbursed and not just a quick online tutorial.

Like the Credit CARD Act of 2009,[28] which requires clear credit card disclosures, student loans should come with:

- Personalized repayment tables
- Interest and amortization schedules
- A required acknowledgment of the financial impact

I've always said that students don't know what they don't know. Unfortunately, by the time they find out they have borrowed too much, it is too late.

Real Experience

> "I was told I 'qualified' for $20,000 per semester when I only needed $3,000-$4,000. No financial counseling was offered. I had to rearrange my work schedule just to avoid taking out more than I needed. Many of my peers weren't so lucky."
>
> **Mindy Lester, PhD**

Each semester in my personal finance class, I invite speakers from the Arkansas Student Loan Authority. It's an eye-opening experience. Many students are stunned to realize how much they've borrowed—and how little they understand about their loan terms.

Some have used student loan funds for spring break trips, vehicles, weddings, and luxury items. Once the money's spent, the regret kicks in—but it's too late.

Not long ago, a personal finance student came to me visibly shaken after class. She had just completed her second year of pharmacy school, with two more to go. During our discussion on student loans, reality hit her hard.

---

28. Federal Trade Commission, *Credit Card Accountability Responsibility and Disclosure Act of 2009 (Credit CARD Act)*, Pub. L. No. 111–24, 123 Stat. 1734, codified in relevant part at 15 U.S.C. §§ 1601–1667f, 1681 et seq., and 1693 et seq., accessed September 4, 2025, https://www.ftc.gov/legal-library/browse/statutes/credit-card-accountability-responsibility-disclosure-act-2009-credit-card-act.

She explained that she lived at home, had no major living expenses, and her only real cost was tuition—about $22,000 per year. But when she started pharmacy school, she was simply told how much she could borrow, not necessarily how much she should. Without understanding the long-term impact, she took out the full loan amount offered each semester.

Now, just halfway through school, she had accumulated nearly $120,000 in student loan debt—most of it at 8–9% interest, compounding daily. Worse yet, she had just received another loan disbursement for the upcoming semester, even though she wouldn't need the funds for another five or six months.

I encouraged her to act immediately: return the unused loan funds to the school and, moving forward, borrow only what was absolutely necessary.

It was a hard lesson, but an important one. Just because you're offered the money doesn't mean you should take it.

After College: Know Your Options

1. Know Your Loans

Start at studentaid.gov. There, you can:

- View all your federal loans
- Check interest rates, servicers, and payment plans
- Review your borrowing history

Ask yourself:

- Are my loans subsidized or unsubsidized?
- What's my current repayment plan?
- When do payments begin?

2. Explore Public Service Loan Forgiveness (PSLF)

If you work for a US federal, state, local, or nonprofit employer, you may qualify for loan forgiveness after 120 payments.

> **BAKER'S CAVEAT:** Paperwork errors are very common. In 2018, 55% of borrowers were denied due to ineligible payments. Another 24% were denied due to incomplete applications.[29]
>
> Check out Temporary Expanded PSLF if you've been previously denied.[30]

3. Consolidation vs. Refinancing

Consolidation *(federal):*

- Combines all federal loans into one
- Makes monthly payments simpler
- May help qualify for PSLF
- Interest rate becomes a weighted average (rounded up)

Refinancing *(private):*

- Replaces your current loan(s) with a new private loan
- May lower your interest rate
- You lose federal protections (like PSLF eligibility or income-driven repayment)

Before Refinancing

- ❍ Compare multiple lenders (try marketplaces like Credible.com).
- ❍ Be sure to check with your state's student loan authority. Many offer private student loans or refinancing options with competitive interest rates. For example, the Arkansas Student Loan Authority provides private refinancing that's often a couple of percentage points lower than national lenders.[31]
- ❍ Watch for hidden fees or early payoff penalties.
- ❍ Don't refinance federal loans if pursuing PSLF.
- ❍ Confirm forgiveness terms for death/disability (federal loans include this—many private ones don't).

---

29. Federal Student Aid, *Loan Forgiveness Data Center*, U.S. Department of Education, accessed September 5, 2025, https://studentaid.gov/data-center/student/loan-forgiveness.

30. Federal Student Aid, *Public Service Loan Forgiveness (PSLF)*, U.S. Department of Education, accessed September 5, 2025, https://studentaid.gov/manage-loans/forgiveness-cancellation/public-service.

31. Richard Richtmyer, "Compare the Best Private Student Loans for September 2025 in Minutes," *Credible*, September 2, 2025, https://www.credible.com/student-loans.

4. Pay Off Loans *and* Invest

You may ask: Should I pay off loans or contribute to retirement?

Here's a quick framework:

- Always contribute enough to your 401(k) to get the full employer match, because it's free money.
- Paying down a loan with 6–7% interest = a *guaranteed* 6–7% equivalent.
- Consider splitting additional money between loan payoff and retirement savings.

If you live below your means and resist lifestyle creep, you *can* do both. I have former personal finance students who paid off six-figure loans in just a few years. You can do it too, and it will transform your financial future!

Student Loan Survival Kit: 7 Quick Wins

1. **Know your loan**. Check your loan details at studentaid.gov.
2. **Don't borrow blindly**. Understand how much you'll owe *and for how long*.
3. **Only borrow what you need**. Not what you "qualify" for.
4. **Avoid lifestyle creep**. Loans aren't for spring break or new trucks.
5. **Explore PSLF or forgiveness programs.** And do it early.
6. **Never skip your employer 401(k) match**. It's free money.
7. **Refinance smartly**. Only if it saves you interest *and* you don't need federal protections.

DR. SARAH GRIFFIN, PHARMD: Paying It Off Smart: How I Beat $80k in Student Loans Fast

I was fortunate to graduate from undergrad debt-free, but pharmacy school was a different story. Between tuition, fees, and living expenses, I ended up with about $80,000 in student loans. Even while in school, I worked 10 to 20 hours a week during the semesters and full time in the summers. I saved most of what I earned but still made room for the occasional splurge and fun with friends.

After graduation, I made a decision that helped me pay off my loans in just two and a half years. I didn't consolidate them; instead, I targeted the unsubsidized and higher-interest loans first. During my residency year, I managed to save enough to pay off all the interest that had accrued, which was about $4,000 to $5,000, so that once I started making payments, they went directly toward the principal.

I kept living like a resident for two years after residency, which allowed me to stay focused and knock out the debt fast. I often share this strategy with students: live lean early, hit the principal hard, and save yourself thousands in the long run.

The personal finance lessons I learned helped shape the rest of my financial life, too. I bought a home with a low-interest mortgage, paid off my car in under two years, and have still been able to travel, including a few international trips. I use credit cards strategically for cash back and rewards but always pay the balance in full each month.

Most importantly, getting control of my finances has allowed me to give generously to my church, to scholarships, and to mission work I care deeply about. Being smart with money doesn't mean giving up joy; it just means being intentional. And I've found that it's one of the most freeing things you can do.

PRINCIPLE #7

Drive a Car—Don't Let It Drive Your Identity

Social media has given us front-row seats to curated versions of people's lives that are filtered and polished for maximum impact. It's become second nature to scroll through feeds filled with exotic getaways, designer meals, and luxury lifestyles.

"Keeping up with the Joneses" has evolved into "keeping up with the Kardashians," and now it's turned into trying to keep up with strangers on Instagram—most of whom we've never met.

But here's the warning: Don't confuse the illusion of wealth with actual wealth.

It's easy to fall into the trap of defining success by material things. We wrap our identity in the car we drive, the clothes we wear, and the home we live in. But those things can easily become barriers to building real wealth, especially a car.

A vehicle, while often seen as a status symbol, is one of the biggest roadblocks to financial independence. It's not just transportation anymore—it's an emotional purchase. I tell my finance students all the time:

"There's no parade from your driveway to the office to show off your car."

Go back to Baker's Dirty Dozen Principle #1: If buying a luxury vehicle makes you feel validated, that's understandable, but be honest about why you're buying it. And don't forget Principle #3: A car is a depreciating asset. It loses value the moment you drive it off the lot and offers little to no return on your investment.

This isn't to say you should never enjoy luxury. One day, you absolutely can. But that day should come when:

- You're debt-free (excluding possibly your mortgage)
- You're consistently saving for retirement
- Your financial goals are on track

FINANCING A VEHICLE: WHEN (AND WHEN NOT) TO DO IT

There are very few situations where I'd recommend financing a car. One of them is when you're fresh out of college, just starting your career, and need a safe, reliable vehicle to get to work. Even then, it should be a thoughtful decision, and not an emotional one.

Let's walk through two choices and the opportunity cost that comes with each.

Car Buying Choices: More Than a Monthly Payment

Let's compare three car buying scenarios and the long-term opportunity cost of each decision.

Choice #1: The "Reward Yourself" Yukon

- **Vehicle:** New, fully loaded GMC Yukon 4x4
- **Price:** $65,000

The Voice in Your Head Says: "You've earned this. After years of college and graduate school, you deserve a vehicle that reflects your success."

The Salesman Says: "You can totally afford the monthly payments."

Lifestyle Creep Translation: You're buying an image, not just transportation.

Choice #2: The Reliable Toyota Corolla

- **Vehicle:** New Toyota Corolla with premium features
- **Price:** $25,000

What You Gain: A dependable, safe, and stylish ride—without derailing your financial goals.

Opportunity Cost: Investing the $40,000 Difference

If you invested the $40,000 difference into a stock index mutual fund or ETF earning an average annual return of 8% (compounded annually):

Year	Account Value
5	$58,773
10	$86,357
25	$273,939
30	$402,506

That's almost half a million dollars from one car-buying decision. Not a bad return for driving something slightly more modest.

Choice #3: The "Keep It Simple" Used Car

- **Vehicle:** 5-year-old Toyota Camry or Nissan Altima with ~60k miles
- **Price:** $15,000

Difference from Choice #1: $50,000

Opportunity Cost of Choice #3

If you invested the $50,000 savings with the same 8% return:

Year	Account Value
5	$73,466
10	$107,946
25	$342,242
30	$503,133

If those numbers made your brain short-circuit, you're not alone. These are the kinds of decisions that quietly build wealth over time.[1]

Baker's Takeaway

My goal isn't to tell you what car to buy. If owning a more expensive vehicle genuinely fulfills you, that's your choice. But I want you to clearly understand the opportunity cost of that decision.

Would you rather enjoy the thrill of a $65,000 SUV or sports car today, or build $400,000+ in investments to fuel travel, home upgrades, or an early, comfortable retirement down the road?

Remember Baker's Dirty Dozen Principle #1: Find a path that will truly fulfill you. Smart financial choices open doors to the things that matter most.

Also keep in mind: more expensive vehicles come with higher insurance, maintenance, registration, and tax costs. That $65,000 SUV doesn't just cost more up front, but it keeps costing you.

Next up, some practical car buying tips from a former student, Grant Florer, who did the research and shares what every buyer should know.

───── **DR. GRANT FLORER:** How Not to Get Fleeced on Four Wheels ─────

Let's start with the basics. Most car buyers fall into one of two camps:

1. *"I just need a car!"* (usually ends in regret and ramen dinners)
2. *"Let's make a smart decision that I won't hate tomorrow."*

This guide is for Camp #2. If you're in Camp #1 . . . may the odds be ever in your favor.

Used or New? That Is the Question.

Used cars are like rescue dogs: they've been around, might have a few quirks, but can be loyal, affordable, and love you forever (or at least for 100,000 miles).

New cars? You get the honor of being the first to drop french fries between the seats. But the second you drive off the lot, you lose thousands in

---

1. Calculations made at: Calculator.net, *Investment Calculator*, accessed September 5, 2025, https://www.calculator.net/investment-calculator.html.

value. It's like buying a banana at peak ripeness only to watch it go brown on the ride home.

Used = smarter value. Just buy the *right* used car.

How to Be a Used-Car Ninja

Step 1: Don't Buy a Headache

Avoid cars with:

- High mileage and sketchy maintenance history
- "Salvage" titles (unless you like playing mechanical roulette)
- Luxury badges—their repairs are the stuff of nightmares
- Out-of-warranty European models—$1,200 for a window switch is *not* a flex

Step 2: Reliability > Flashy Tech

That 2014 Toyota might not have Apple CarPlay, but it *will* start on cold mornings when your neighbor's BMW is in the shop.

Stick to proven names: Toyota, Honda, Mazda, Subaru (just skip the head gasket drama years—Google it).

Grant's "Nice Used Car" Formula

- Age: 3–7 years old
- Mileage: 10,000–15,000 per year (5-year-old car = 50k–75k)
- Buy from: Private sellers or small dealerships
- Avoid: Big dealers and Carvana; you're paying for their espresso machine

Negotiation 101: The Dance of Mutual Suspicion

- Never show excitement. Be cool. Mysterious. Like you're auditioning for *Top Gear*.
- Test drive—and not just around the block. Drive it like you're already regretting the payments.
- Always get a mechanic's inspection. Think of it as a pre-nup for your engine.

When It's Time to Talk Money

- Start lower than you're willing to go. Leave room to "meet in the middle."
- Don't over-haggle on a great deal. Good cars go fast.
- If it feels sketchy—bounce. There are more cars than honest sellers.

Red Flags: Run, Don't Drive

- "Clean title," but priced suspiciously low
- Seller refuses outside inspection
- Dash lights up like a Vegas casino
- "Just needs a little work" = it's practically a parts donor

Final Tips for the Frugal and Wise

- Cash talks. Flashing bills is like flirting in a rom-com—things get easier real quick.
- Skip warranties and upsells. They're dealer moneymakers, not buyer protection.
- Bring backup. A car-savvy friend or a naturally suspicious one. Bonus if they're both.

What Grant Drives (Because You Gotta Walk the Talk)

A 2010 Toyota Highlander, bought for $9,500 in 2021.120,000 miles. Runs like a dream. No issues. Basically the golden retriever of cars.

Baker's Dirty Dozen
PRINCIPLE #8

Stocks, Bonds, and Cash—Oh My!

"Success in investing doesn't correlate with IQ ... what
you need is the temperament to control the urges that
get other people into trouble in investing."

Warren Buffett

Thank goodness investing isn't tied to IQ, otherwise, I'd be in serious trouble. Turns out, patience beats genius . . . and that's the only race I've ever had a shot at winning.

Today, buying and selling stocks is as simple as a few taps on your smartphone. Trades happen in real time, with no need to call a stockbroker or wait for confirmation by mail like in the old days.

MIKE RYBURN: The $6,000 Oops

My brother-in-law, Mike Ryburn, once got a hot stock tip in the '70s: Worthen Banking Corporation was a solid buy at $7.50 a share. Thinking $750 was a reasonable gamble, he picked up the phone (yes, the kind attached to a wall) and called his stockbroker, back when you actually had to talk to someone to buy stocks.

Mike said, "I'd like to buy 'a hundred shares' of Worthen."
The broker heard, "Eight hundred shares."

A few days later, Mike opened his mailbox, took one look at the trade confirmation, and nearly needed CPR. Instead of $750, he had accidentally bought $6,000 worth of Worthen stock.

He sprinted to the newspaper (this was the '70s—no smartphone apps) to check the stock price. To his shock, Worthen had already nudged up to nearly $8. After a few deep breaths, he shrugged and said, "Well . . . I guess I'll just ride it out."

And ride it out he did.

Worthen was eventually acquired by Boatman's Bancshares, which got scooped up by NationsBank, which merged with—you guessed it—Bank of America. Through mergers and stock splits, Mike's accidental 800 shares multiplied into 2,100 shares of BAC stock.

Today, with BAC trading around $45.00, Mike's $6,000 oops is worth over $94,500. Not bad for a miscommunication.

But here's the thing—you don't need a lucky break (or a misunderstood phone call) to succeed at investing.

As you read Baker's Dirty Dozen Principle #8, my goal is to show you the *old, boring, and proven* approach to building wealth through investing. No gimmicks. No hot tips. Just time-tested strategies that work.

UNDERSTANDING YOUR INVESTMENT OPTIONS

Let's start by reviewing the three most common types of investments, ordered by increasing risk and potential return:

Investment Type	Description	Risk Level
Cash Equivalents	CDs, money market funds, treasury bills	Low
Bonds (Debt)	Government or corporate bonds	Medium
Stocks (Equities)	Ownership in companies (large or small)	High

Understanding how these investments have historically performed can serve as a searchlight to help guide your future financial decisions. Keep the chart below in mind as you read through this chapter.

Understanding Historical Investment Returns

Investing involves balancing risk and reward. By examining historical performance, we can gain insights into how different asset classes have behaved over time.

Common Investment Options

Investments can be broadly categorized based on their risk and return profiles:

- **Cash Equivalents:** Low risk, low return (e.g., treasury bills)
- **Bonds (Debt Instruments):** Moderate risk, moderate return (e.g., government and corporate bonds)
- **Stocks (Equities):** Higher risk, higher return (e.g., large and small company stocks)

Understanding these categories helps investors make informed decisions aligned with their financial goals and risk tolerance.

Historical Returns (1926-2024)

The following table presents the average annual returns of various asset classes over the period from 1928 to 2024:[1,2]

Asset Class	Average Annual Return
Inflation (CPI)	2.90%
Cash Equivalents	3.31%
Bonds (Averaging government and corporate)	4.50%
Large Company Stocks (S&P 500)	9.94%
Small Company Stocks	11.74%

- **Inflation**: Represents the average annual rate at which the general price level for goods and services rises, eroding purchasing power.

1. Ben Carlson, "Historical Returns For Stocks, Bonds, Cash, Real Estate and Gold," *A Wealth of Common Sense*, January 14, 2025, https://awealthofcommonsense.com/2025/01/historical-returns-for-stocks-bonds-cash-real-estate-and-gold.
2. These figures illustrate the trade-off between risk and return: Jonathan Ponciano, "Maximize Your 401(k) Growth: Should You Go All In on Stocks?" *Investopedia*, May 12, 2025, https://www.investopedia.com/maximize-your-401k-8769574?utm.

- **Cash Equivalents like Treasury Bills**: Short-term government securities with minimal risk and modest returns
- **Long-Term Government Bonds**: Debt securities issued by the government with longer maturities, offering higher returns than treasury bills but with increased interest rate risk
- **Long-Term Corporate Bonds**: Debt securities issued by corporations, generally offering higher yields than government bonds due to increased credit risk
- **Large Company Stocks**: Shares of well-established companies, providing substantial returns with moderate volatility
- **Small Company Stocks**: Shares of smaller companies, historically yielding the highest returns but with greater volatility

It's important to note that while stocks have offered higher returns over the long term, they also come with increased risk and short-term volatility. Diversifying investments across different asset classes can help manage risk and achieve a balanced portfolio.

> "Money frees you from doing things you dislike.
> Since I dislike doing nearly everything, money is handy."
>
> **Groucho Marx**

Cash and Cash Equivalents

Cash and cash equivalents are short-term, highly liquid investments, typically with maturities of 90 days or less. These assets are easily converted into cash and are often held for emergency needs or to take advantage of investment opportunities as they arise.

Because of their liquidity and safety, cash equivalents are an essential part of a balanced financial strategy. But remember: the trade-off for that security is very low return.

Quick Overview
- ✓ **Biggest Advantage**: Liquidity (easy to access when needed)
- ✗ **Biggest Disadvantage**: Low rate of return

Examples of Cash and Cash Equivalents

Bank Checking and Savings Accounts (FDIC insured)

- Checking accounts are used for day-to-day spending.
- Savings accounts are designed for storing money and typically earn a slightly higher interest rate than checking.
- Neither are strong investments from a return standpoint, but they're excellent for liquidity and basic savings.

FDIC (Federal Deposit Insurance Corporation) insures deposits up to $250,000 per depositor, per bank.[3]

Money Market Accounts (MMAs) (FDIC insured)

- Interest-bearing accounts offered by banks and credit unions
- May offer higher rates than standard savings accounts
- Often include check-writing or debit card privileges
- Typically have higher minimum balance requirements and some withdrawal restrictions

Don't confuse money market accounts with money market mutual funds, which are different (see below).

Certificates of Deposit (CDs) (FDIC insured)

- CDs are time deposits that offer higher interest rates in exchange for leaving your money untouched for a set period (e.g., 6 months, 18 months, or several years).
- Early withdrawal usually results in a penalty.

Money Market Mutual Funds (NOT FDIC insured, but may be SIPC protected)

- Invest in short-term, high-quality debt instruments (e.g., treasury bills, commercial paper)
- Designed to be low risk and maintain high liquidity
- Often used by investors who need access to their cash soon (e.g., saving for a down payment)

---

3. To learn more, see https://www.fdic.gov.

- Not insured by FDIC, but most are protected by the SIPC (Securities Investor Protection Corporation), which helps safeguard against brokerage firm failure

SIPC protects investments up to $500,000 (including $250,000 for cash), but not against market losses.[4]

> **BAKER'S TIP:** Cash equivalents won't build long-term wealth, but they play a critical role in your overall financial health. Use them for your emergency fund, short-term savings, and as a cushion to cover life's unexpected turns without dipping into long-term investments.

Bonds: Lending with Interest (Not Ownership)

When you purchase a bond, you're essentially lending money to a government (federal, state, or local) or a corporation. In return, the issuer agrees to pay you regular interest (often called the "coupon") and repay the principal at a later date, typically the bond's maturity.

Unlike stocks, owning a bond does not give you any ownership in the company or government entity. You're the lender, not a shareholder.

Advantages of Investing in Bonds

- ✓ **Higher interest rates than cash equivalents** (e.g., savings accounts, CDs, treasury bills)
- ✓ **Lower volatility than stocks**: generally considered a more stable asset class
- ✓ **Tax advantages with certain types** (e.g., municipal bonds are often exempt from federal, and sometimes state/local, taxes)

Disadvantages and Risks of Bonds

✗ **Interest Rate Risk:** Bond prices move inversely with interest rates:

- If interest rates rise, existing bond prices fall.
- If interest rates fall, existing bond prices increase.

---

4. To learn more, see https://www.sipc.org.

✗ Credit (Default) Risk: If a bond issuer cannot make interest or principal payments, they may default. This is more common with lower-rated corporate bonds, but governments have defaulted too. Examples:

- *Corporate:* Enron, Blockbuster
- *Sovereign:* Russia, Argentina (post-2000)
- *US Territory:* Puerto Rico defaulted on $1 billion of general obligation bonds in 2016.[5]

✗ Callable Bond Risk: Some bonds are callable, meaning the issuer can buy them back before maturity, usually after an initial lock-in period.

Example: You buy a 20-year AAA-rated bond paying 4% annually. After 5 years, interest rates fall to 2%. The issuer can "call" the bond back and reissue new ones at the lower rate leaving you with cash to reinvest at a worse return.

Should You Buy Individual Bonds or Bond Mutual Funds?

Like stocks, individual bonds come with more risk due to lack of diversification. Most investors are better off choosing bond mutual funds or ETFs for simplicity and balance.

Advantages of Bond Mutual Funds

- ✓ **Easier to diversify**: Individual bonds often require large minimum investments ($1,000, $5,000, or more).
- ✓ **Professional management**: Fund managers handle the research, selection, and trading of bonds.
- ✓ **Better pricing**: Mutual funds can buy in bulk, often getting better deals than individual investors.
- ✓ **Monthly payouts**: Bond funds typically pay interest monthly (vs. semi-annually for individual bonds), improving cash flow.
- ✓ **Tax-deferred growth**: When held in tax-advantaged accounts like 401(k)s or IRAs, you pay no tax on gains or interest until withdrawal.

---

5. Michelle Kaske, "Puerto Rico Says It Will Default Even With Congressional Aid," *ThinkAdvisor*, June 29, 2016, https://www.thinkadvisor.com/2016/06/29/puerto-rico-says-it-will-default-even-with-congressional-aid.

> **BAKER'S CHOICE:** For most people, bond mutual funds are the way to go. They offer better diversification, easier access, and less hassle.
>
> I've only purchased two individual bonds in my life: a State of Arkansas College Savings Bond over thirty years ago, and a set of US government I Bonds a few years back that were earning around 9% interest. Both were unique opportunities, and I haven't repeated either since.

Stocks: Owning a Piece of the Action

When you buy stock, you're buying ownership in a company. Own a hundred shares of Walmart (ticker symbol: WMT)? Congratulations! You're a part-owner of Walmart. Technically, you have voting rights and can even attend shareholder meetings in Bentonville, Arkansas. In fact, you could walk into a local store and say, "Hi, I'm one of the owners of Walmart. Just browsing."

Will they call security? Maybe. But it wouldn't be a lie.

How Do You Make Money from Stocks?

There are two main ways to profit from owning stocks:

1. Stock Appreciation

When a company performs well (or is expected to), its stock price often rises due to increased demand. You can sell shares for a profit if the price goes up after your purchase. You only make a profit or a loss when you sell your stock. I often hear well-educated people say, "I lost $1,000 in the market today." But that statement only holds true if they actually sold their stocks at a loss. Until you sell, gains and losses are just on paper. Nothing is truly gained or lost until a sale is made.

2. Dividends

This is your share of the profits. Companies like Starbucks (SBUX), Coca-Cola (KO), and Procter & Gamble (PG) often pay shareholders a quarterly dividend—literally a check in the mail (or direct deposit) as a thank-you for being an owner.

Not all companies pay dividends, especially newer, fast-growing companies that reinvest profits into growth.

Advantages of Owning Stocks

✓ **Highest long-term return potential** among common investment options (stocks, bonds, and cash equivalents)
✓ **Pride in owning companies you believe in**
✓ **Excitement of watching your shares grow**, which makes for a great conversation starter

Disadvantages and Risks of Owning Stocks

✗ **High Risk, High Reward:** Individual stocks offer no guarantees. The potential for higher returns also comes with greater volatility.

✗ **Lack of Diversification:** If you only own stock in one company, your financial fate is tied to its success—or failure. For example, during the COVID-19 pandemic, oil company stocks plummeted as oil prices temporarily went negative.

✗ **Bankruptcy Happens:** Companies can and do go out of business. Some memorable examples:

- *Blockbuster (BBI) and Movie Gallery (MOVI):* In the 1990s, these video rental giants dominated. But Blockbuster infamously passed on buying Netflix for $50 million in 2000. Netflix later revolutionized video streaming, while both Blockbuster and Movie Gallery filed for bankruptcy.
- *Enron (ENE):* Once a booming energy company, Enron collapsed in 2001 after an enormous accounting scandal. The stock became worthless almost overnight.

Real-Life Example: Selling at the Right Time

My friend Vince Insalaco recognized the video rental trend in the 1980s and opened a chain of Family Video stores across Arkansas, Missouri, and Oklahoma. He built it to 52 locations.

But Vince also had vision. Sensing the coming shift to digital streaming, he sold his entire chain to Movie Gallery in 2002, just a few years before Movie Gallery went out of business.

So, How Should You Invest in Stocks?

There's a time and place for buying individual stocks, especially dividend-producing blue chips.

But for most investors, especially beginners, the best approach is to invest in stock mutual funds or ETFs, especially in retirement accounts like a 401(k), 403(b), or Roth IRA.

For example: If your 401(k) offers a fund like Vanguard Dividend Growth (VDIGX), you're buying into a professionally managed portfolio that holds shares in hundreds of companies—like Microsoft (MSFT), McDonald's (MCD), and Johnson & Johnson (JNJ).

This diversification means that even if one company, say, Enron or Blockbuster, fails, your overall investment isn't wiped out.

What's the S&P 500 I've Heard So Much About?

The S&P 500 Index is a market index that tracks the 500 largest US publicly traded companies. It's one of the most reliable indicators of large-cap US stock market performance.

Other major indexes include the Dow Jones Industrial Average, which tracks just 30 companies, and the Nasdaq Composite, which skews toward tech.

> **BAKER'S TAKEAWAY:** Buying individual stocks can be exciting, and even rewarding. But it's also risky. For most investors, diversified funds like index funds or dividend mutual funds are the safer, smarter path.

"Money isn't everything, but it sure keeps
you in touch with your children."

J. P. Getty

Mutual Funds and ETFs: Diversified Investing Made Simple

Mutual funds and Exchange-Traded Funds (ETFs) are two of the most popular investment vehicles for everyday investors. They allow you to pool your money with other investors to buy a broad mix of assets, like stocks, bonds, or cash equivalents, without having to pick individual investments yourself.

While similar in many ways, there are some key differences worth noting.

Key Differences Between Mutual Funds and ETFs

Feature	Mutual Funds	ETFs
Management Style	Typically actively managed	Usually passively managed (index-based)
Pricing	Traded once per day (end of day NAV)	Traded throughout the day like a stock
Expense Ratios	Generally higher	Typically lower
Tax Efficiency	Can be less tax-efficient	More tax-efficient due to trading structure
Minimum Investment	Often requires a minimum amount	Can buy as little as one share

Real-Life Comparison

Consider two similar funds from Vanguard:

- **Vanguard 500 Index Mutual Fund Admiral Shares (VFIAX):** Expense ratio: 0.04%
- **Vanguard S&P 500 ETF (VOO):** Expense ratio: 0.03%

Both follow the same benchmark index—the S&P 500—and have nearly identical portfolios. The primary differences are in management style, expense ratio, and how they are bought or sold.[6]

---

6. Want to learn more? See this comparison on Vanguard's website: "ETFs vs. Mutual Funds: A Comparison," *Vanguard*, https://investor.vanguard.com/investor-resources-education/etfs/etf-vs-mutual-fund.

How Mutual Funds and ETFs Work

When you invest in a mutual fund or ETF, your money is pooled with others to buy a wide range of securities. This gives you:

- **Diversification** without needing to hand-pick individual stocks or bonds
- **Professional management**, especially with actively managed funds
- **Access to a range of investment strategies** (e.g., growth, value, income, etc.)

You can invest in these funds through:

- Your employer-sponsored retirement plan (401(k), 403(b), etc.)
- An Individual Retirement Account (IRA and Roth IRA)
- A taxable brokerage account

Advantages of Mutual Funds and ETFs

- ✓ **Simplicity:** You don't need to pick individual stocks or monitor the market daily.
- ✓ **Diversification:** Your investment is spread across dozens or even hundreds of securities.
- ✓ **Professional Management:** Fund managers handle buying/selling based on the fund's goals.
- ✓ **Access to a Variety of Goals:** Funds can target growth, income, or tax efficiency.
- ✓ **Flexible Investing:** Suitable for retirement, education savings (529 plans), or general wealth-building.

If you invest outside of a tax-advantaged account, keep good records and consider hiring a CPA or Enrolled Agent to help you navigate tax reporting.

Things to Consider

- ✗ **Fees:** Mutual funds may charge management fees, marketing fees (12b-1), and other expenses. ETFs generally have lower expense ratios.

✗ **Commissions:** Some funds still charge commissions (though many brokerage platforms offer no-fee investing).

✗ **Trading Limitations:** Mutual funds trade once per day. ETFs trade like stocks.

Types of Mutual Funds and ETFs

There are thousands of mutual funds and ETFs to choose from. Fortunately, your main selection will often come from your employer-sponsored plan, which typically offers 20–35 curated options.

According to a recent survey:

- Total number of US mutual funds (as of 2023): 7,222, managing $21.7 trillion in assets
- Total number of US ETFs (as of 2023): 3,637, managing $10.3 trillion in assets[7]

Common types include:

- Money Market Funds
- Stock Growth Funds
- Stock Value Funds
- Aggressive Growth Funds
- Stock Index Funds (e.g., S&P 500)
- Balanced Funds (stocks and bonds)
- Target-Date Retirement Funds
- Taxable and Tax-Exempt Income Funds
- International and Global Funds
- Alternative Funds[8]

---

7. Investment Company Institute, *The US ETF Market: Frequently Asked Questions*, updated April 28, 2025, accessed September 8, 2025, https://www.ici.org/faqs/faqs_etfs_market.

8. For definitions and examples of these fund types and others, see Adam Hayes, "Investing in Mutual Funds: What They Are and How They Work," *Investopedia*, August 29, 2025, https://www.investopedia.com/terms/m/mutualfund.asp#toc-types-of-mutual-funds.

> **BAKER'S TAKEAWAY:** Mutual funds and ETFs are powerful tools for investors at any level. Whether you're saving for retirement, funding a child's education, or seeking tax-efficient investing, these vehicles offer simplicity, diversification, and professional guidance.
>
> Rather than putting all your eggs in one basket (say, buying $1,000 of Amazon stock), you can buy a diversified fund that owns hundreds of companies, including Amazon, spreading your risk and increasing your potential for long-term success.

Mutual Fund and ETF Fees: What You Don't Know *Will* Cost You

When choosing between mutual funds or ETFs—whether in your 401(k), 403(b), Roth IRA, or other investment accounts—fees matter. In fact, fees can be one of the most important predictors of a fund's long-term performance.

Types of Common Fees

Before choosing a fund, make sure you understand the following fee types:

1. **Sales Charges / Commissions (Loads)**
   - *Front-end load*: Fee charged when you buy the fund
   - *Back-end load*: Fee charged when you sell
   - *No-load funds*: No commission fees (generally preferred)

2. **Expense Ratio**
   - This is the annual fee, expressed as a percentage, that covers fund management and administrative costs. Lower is generally better.

3. **12b-1 Fees**
   - A type of marketing and distribution fee, sometimes included in the expense ratio. These are considered less investor-friendly and should be avoided when possible.

Do Fees Really Matter?

At first glance, a 1.5% annual fee might not seem significantly worse than a 0.2% fee—but over time, the difference is staggering.

Assume the only difference between two investments is the expense ratio. If you invested for several decades, the lower-cost fund could result in hundreds of thousands more in savings.

Lower Fees = More $$ Staying Invested = Greater Potential Growth

> **BAKER'S CAVEAT:** Keep a close eye on the fees associated with mutual funds and ETFs in your employer-sponsored retirement plan. Many plans offer low-cost index funds or target-date funds with expense ratios under 0.2%. If your plan includes higher-fee options, understand why and what you're getting in return.

RETIREMENT PLANS: A SYSTEM TRANSFORMED

Retirement in America has undergone a massive transformation over the past few decades. What was once a relatively predictable and secure phase of life has become more uncertain and more self-directed. The biggest shift? A move away from defined benefit plans—traditional pensions—to defined contribution plans, like 401(k)s.

For much of the 20th century, many American workers could count on a pension. These defined benefit plans guaranteed a specific monthly income in retirement, usually based on salary history and years of service. Stay with a company for 30 years, and you could retire with a reliable income for life. It was simple, and it worked, for a while.

But times have changed. Maintaining these plans became increasingly expensive for employers. As the workforce became more mobile, and as global competition and government regulations grew more complex, pensions began to disappear.

In 1998, 59% of Fortune 500 companies offered defined benefit pension plans to new hires. By 2019, that number had plummeted to just 14%. This sharp decline reflects a widespread shift away from traditional pensions toward defined contribution plans like 401(k)s, which are simpler to administer and more cost-effective for employers.[9]

What Is a Defined Benefit Plan?

A defined benefit plan provides a fixed retirement benefit, usually paid monthly, that is calculated based on your earnings history and length of employment. These plans are entirely employer-sponsored, and they shift both the investment and longevity risk away from the employee. While generous, they are also complex and costly to administer.

That's why they're becoming rare.

The New Standard: Defined Contribution Plans

In place of pensions, the dominant model today is the defined contribution plan, most commonly the 401(k). In these plans, employees set aside a portion of their paycheck into an investment account, often with a company match. Unlike pensions, the benefit at retirement isn't guaranteed. Instead, it depends on how much you contribute, how your investments perform, and how long you let it grow.

These plans are more flexible, portable, and employer-friendly, but they also place more responsibility on the individual. You're in charge of your own retirement future.

Key Characteristics of Defined Contribution Plans

- Funded primarily by the employee (with optional employer matching)
- Typically tax-deferred (you don't pay taxes until withdrawal)
- Subject to contribution limits and withdrawal rules
- No guaranteed payout—your balance depends on market performance

This shift from defined benefit to defined contribution has redefined retirement. Today, planning for retirement means understanding your plan

---

9. Jane Their, "AARP is recruiting Gen Z in an unconventional way—with a pension: We tell them it's 'free money,'" *Fortune*, May 17, 2023, https://fortune.com/2023/05/17/aarp-offering-pension-recruiting-gen-z.

options, taking advantage of any employer matches, and contributing consistently, even early in your career.

Defined contribution plan examples include: Traditional 401(k), Roth 401(k), Traditional 403(b), Roth 403(b) TSP and Roth TSP

The Traditional 401(k): A Powerful Tool for Retirement

The traditional 401(k) is one of the most powerful tools available for building retirement wealth, and it's one you'll likely encounter early in your career. For this section, we'll use the term *traditional 401(k)* to also include traditional 403(b) plans (used by nonprofits) and Thrift Savings Plans (TSPs) for federal employees and military members. They operate similarly and follow many of the same rules.

How It Works

A traditional 401(k) is a defined contribution plan sponsored by your employer. You contribute a portion of your pre-tax income into a retirement account that grows over time. Your employer may also chip in through a matching contribution, which we'll cover in detail in a moment.

These contributions:

- Lower your taxable income in the year you contribute.
- Grow tax-deferred: you don't pay taxes on investment gains until you withdraw the money.
- Become taxable income when withdrawn after age 59½.

Example: Jack B. Nimble

Jack earns $60,000 and contributes $10,000 to his traditional 401(k). He only pays income tax on $50,000 this year. His $10,000 grows tax-free until retirement, and then it's taxed when withdrawn.

Contribution Limits and Investment Options

Each year, the IRS sets limits on how much you can contribute. For 2025:

- The maximum employee contribution is $23,500.
- If you're over age 50, you can contribute an additional $7,500 (called a "catch-up" contribution).

Employers often offer around 25–30 investment options, including:

- Stock mutual funds
- Bond funds
- Target-date funds
- Stable value or money market funds

You decide how your money is allocated, and it pays to get educated.

The Employer Match: Free Money (Seriously)

Employer matching is one of the biggest perks of a 401(k). It's essentially free money, but many employees leave it on the table.

Example: Chuck Waggon

Chuck works at Brister Manufacturing, which matches 100% of the first 5% of employee contributions. Chuck earns $50,000 and contributes 5% ($2,500) of his salary. Brister matches that $2,500, bringing his total annual contribution to $5,000.

Using the assumptions of no salary increases and an 8% rate of return, his 401(k) balance could look like:

- After 25 years: $380,151
- After 30 years: $589,073

Note: Assumes monthly contributions, 8% return, and no early withdrawals.[10]

---

10. Calculations made at: https://www.bankrate.com/retirement/401-k-or-roth-ira-calculator/
https://www.calculator.net/401k-calculator.html.

The Tax Advantage

Here's a simple breakdown of how a traditional 401(k) contribution affects your paycheck:

	With 401(k) (10%)	Without 401(k)
Gross Pay	$100,000	$100,000
401(k) Contribution	$10,000	N/A
Taxable Income	$90,000	$100,000
Federal Tax	$11,700 (est.)	$13,000 (est.)
FICA/Medicare	$6,885	$7,650
Take-Home Pay	$71,415	$79,350

Note: Assumes single filer, 13% federal tax rate, 7.65% FICA/Medicare, and no state income tax.

Even though you're saving $10,000 for retirement, your paycheck only goes down by $7,935. That's the power of pre-tax savings.

But Wait—The IRS Still Gets Paid

Just because your taxes are deferred doesn't mean they're avoided. When you retire and begin taking withdrawals after age 59½, you'll pay taxes at whatever your tax rate is at that time. This is why the IRS is happy to give you a break today, because they'll still collect down the road.

Are People Saving Enough?

Sadly, no. Most Americans aren't contributing nearly enough to their 401(k)s. Here's what the average and median balances look like by age:[11]

Age Group	Average	Median
Under 25	$7,351	$2,816
25–34	$37,557	$14,933
35–44	$91,281	$35,537
45–54	$168,646	$60,763
55–64	$244,750	$87,571
65+	$272,588	$88,488

11. Brian Baker, "The average 401(k) balance by age: See how you compare," *Bankrate,* September 3, 2025, https://www.bankrate.com/retirement/average-401k-balance-by-age/.

The median (middle value) is much lower than the average because a small percentage of high savers drive the average up. That means *most* people have even less than the figures shown.

So . . . How Much Do You Need?

There's no magic number, but Fidelity suggests aiming for 10x your salary by age 67. That's just a starting point. Your personal goal depends on:

- Health care costs
- Inflation
- Lifestyle
- Social Security benefits
- Whether you own or rent
- And more

In short: Save as much as you reasonably can. If you save "too much," you'll leave a greater legacy—hello, Principle #13.

The Roth 401(k): Tax-Free Growth for Your Future

As tax laws have evolved, so have your retirement options. One of the most powerful, and sometimes underutilized, options is the Roth 401(k). Unlike a traditional 401(k), which gives you a tax break today, the Roth version gives you a tax break later, when you're likely to need it more.

What Is a Roth 401(k)?

A Roth 401(k) is an employer-sponsored retirement account that's funded with after-tax dollars. This means you pay taxes *now* on the money you contribute. In exchange, your money grows tax-free, and when you withdraw it in retirement, neither the contributions nor the earnings are taxed.

If you think you'll be in a higher tax bracket when you retire (or if you just like the idea of tax-free income), a Roth 401(k) could be a smart move.

> **NOTE:** Roth 403(b) plans and Roth TSPs are also available for employees at nonprofits and the federal government, respectively.

Key Features of a Roth 401(k)

- Contributions are taxed up front, not when withdrawn.
- Qualified withdrawals are 100% tax-free after age 59½ and if the account is at least five years old.
- Contribution limits are the same as traditional 401(k)s: $23,500 in 2025 (plus $7,500 catch-up for age 50+).
- Your employer can still match your contributions—but their match goes into a traditional 401(k) account (which will be taxed later).

Example: Mr. Bo Jangles

Bo works at *Macedonia Mad Hatter Haberdashery*, which offers both traditional and Roth 401(k) plans. Bo believes tax rates will rise by the time he retires, so he chooses the Roth 401(k) for tax-free withdrawals in the future.

- Salary: $80,000
- Employee Contribution (10%): $8,000
- Employer Match (100% of first 5%): $4,000
- Total Annual Contribution: $12,000

With an 8% average annual return, Bo's projected retirement balance after 30 years:[12]

- Roth (tax-free portion): $906,266
- Traditional (employer match portion, taxable): $453,133
- Total Balance: $1,359,399

Why Consider a Roth 401(k)?

It all comes down to tax timing.

Right now, tax rates are near historical lows. But with growing national debt and shifting policies, there's a good chance they'll go up in the future. Take a look at some history:

- During WWII, the top tax bracket hit 94%.
- Through the 1950s to the 1970s, it never dropped below 70%.
- In 2018, the top bracket was just 37%.

---

12. All calculations based on monthly contributions using that trusty Texas Instruments BA-35 calculator.

If you believe higher tax rates are on the horizon, paying taxes now (via a Roth 401[k]) might save you a lot in the long run.

Traditional vs. Roth 401(k): Which Should You Choose?

This isn't a one-size-fits-all decision. It depends on your income, your tax bracket now vs. in retirement, and your long-term goals.

Here's how to think about it:

- **Traditional 401(k):** Get the tax break now; pay taxes later.
- **Roth 401(k):** Pay taxes now; enjoy tax-free withdrawals later.

You don't have to pick just one. Many people split their contributions 50/50 between both accounts if their employer allows. Others use a traditional 401(k) to get the upfront break, then contribute to a Roth IRA for the back-end tax benefit.

Either way, doing something is better than doing nothing. Start where you are and adjust as you go.

Side-by-Side Example: Traditional vs. Roth

Let's compare two hypothetical retirement paths using Bankrate's online calculator:[13]

	Traditional 401(k)	Roth 401(k)
Starting Age	30	30
Retirement Age	60	60
Annual Contribution	$12,000	$12,000
Return (avg.)	7%	7%
Current Tax Rate	25%	25%
Account Value	$1,213,615	$1,176,065
Tax on Withdrawals	Yes	No

At first glance, the traditional account appears to win—until you realize the Roth account's full balance is tax-free. That changes the math in a big way.

---

13. You can run your own numbers using Bankrate's 401(k) comparison calculator: "Traditional 401(k) Or Roth 401(k) Calculator," *Bankrate*, https://www.bankrate.com/retirement/401-k-or-roth-ira-calculator/.

What Happens to Your 401(k) When You Leave a Job?

So, you're thinking about leaving your job, or maybe you already did. Whether you're pursuing a new opportunity or running for the hills, one question always comes up:

"What do I do with my 401(k) (or 403(b), TSP, etc.) now?"

Good news: You have options. Let's break them down.

Your Four Options When Changing Jobs

1. Leave It with Your Old Employer.

If you like the investment options and fee structure, you can keep your money where it is. But be aware:

- ✗ Fewer investment choices
- ✗ Possibly higher fees
- ✗ You're no longer an employee, so it can feel disconnected

> **BAKER'S TAKE:** I've never loved the idea of leaving my money with a past employer. Regulations protect your account, but I'd rather have control over it.

2. Roll It into Your New Employer's Plan.

If your new job offers a retirement plan, you might be able to roll your old account into it. This keeps your retirement funds consolidated in one place.

Pros
- ✓ Simplicity
- ✓ All your retirement money in one bucket

Cons
- ✗ Limited investment options
- ✗ Potentially higher fees than doing it yourself

3. Move It to a Rollover IRA. **Baker's Choice!**

This is my go-to option. A rollover IRA gives you full control and access to a much wider variety of investments, including index funds, ETFs, CDs, and even individual stocks.

How to do it:

1. Open a rollover IRA at a brokerage like Fidelity or Schwab. You can also open a Rollover IRA with a mutual fund like Vanguard.
2. Contact your old 401(k) provider to initiate the transfer.
3. Pick your new investments (we'll talk more about options later in the book).

> **IMPORTANT:** Always request a trustee-to-trustee transfer (also called a direct rollover) to avoid taxes or penalties.
>
> **TIMING TIP:** If you have to sell investments before rolling over your account, try not to do it during a market downturn. If possible, wait for a rebound to avoid locking in losses.

4. Cash Out (a.k.a. The Worst Option)

You can take the money and run, but you'll likely pay income taxes *and* a 10% early withdrawal penalty if you're under 59½.

> **BOTTOM LINE:** Cashing out is usually a short-term solution with long-term regrets.
>
> **BAKER'S CHOICE:** Assuming you're in your 20s, 30s, or 40s—you'll likely change jobs several times. Each time, consider rolling your old retirement account into a self-directed rollover IRA. It puts you in the driver's seat with lower fees and better investment options.

What Happens to Your 401(k) When You Die?

Don't worry, it doesn't go to the IRS or to your old boss.

Correct Answer: It goes to the beneficiary you listed on your plan—your spouse, kids, best friend, or cat (okay, maybe not the cat unless you've got a fancy trust in place).

Just be sure to keep your beneficiary information updated, especially after major life changes like marriage, divorce, or the arrival of tiny humans.

What About Employer Contributions?

Glad you asked. Your 401(k) typically has two parts:

1. **Your contributions**: You're always 100% vested. That means you fully own this money right away.
2. **Employer contributions:** These may have a vesting schedule.

Vesting means "ownership over time." For example, your employer might require you to stay three years before you're entitled to 100% of their match.

If you leave early, you might lose part, or all, of the match.

The 401(k), 403(b), and TSP plans we've covered so far are employer-sponsored. But what if you want to save outside of work, or you're self-employed?

Don't worry, we've got you covered. Coming up: Roth and Traditional IRAs.

Individual Retirement Plans (IRAs)

Say it with me 10 times: *"These are individual retirement plans!"*

Seriously, don't confuse them with employer-sponsored plans like 401(k)s or 403(b)s. You'd be surprised how many finance students (and professionals!) mix them up.

Can I Have Both an IRA and a 401(k)?

Yes, you can! Having a 401(k) through your job doesn't disqualify you from also contributing to an IRA. However, your ability to deduct your traditional IRA contributions on your taxes might depend on your income.

Let's break it down:

Traditional IRA

A Traditional IRA is a retirement account that *you* set up and control. It's not tied to your employer. It offers two big benefits:

- ✓ Potential tax deduction on contributions
- ✓ Tax-deferred growth (you don't pay taxes until you withdraw in retirement)

2025 Contribution Limits

- Under age 50: $7,000
- Age 50 or older: $8,000 (thanks to a "catch-up" provision)

These limits apply across all IRAs combined (Traditional + Roth). You can split your contributions, but the total can't exceed the annual cap.

Who Can Deduct Contributions?

Whether your Traditional IRA contributions are fully deductible depends on two things:

1. Do you (or your spouse) have a workplace retirement plan?

- If neither of you has a retirement plan at work, then you can deduct the full amount—no matter your income.
- If you or your spouse *do* have a workplace plan (like a 401(k)), then your income matters.

2. What's your income?

Here are the 2025 modified adjusted gross income limits for deducting Traditional IRA contributions during tax filing:[14]

---

14. Chart Source: Darrow Wealth Management, Boston, MA, https://darrowwealthmanagement.com/blog/2025-contribution-limits-tax-brackets/

Deductible IRA Income Limits (2025)	If you/spouse ARE covered by an employer retirement plan at any point during the year		If you/spouse ARE NOT covered by an employer retirement plan at any point during the year	
	Single	Married filing jointly	Single or married filing jointly (neither spouse covered)	Married filing jointly (one spouse covered)
Full	<$79,000	<$126,000	Any	<$236,000
Partial Tax Deduction	$79,000–$89,000	$126,000–$146,000		$236,000–$246,000
Non-deductible	$89,000+	$146,000+		$246,000+

Summary: Why Consider a Traditional IRA?

- You want additional tax-deferred savings
- You might qualify for a deduction
- You want more control over your investments (especially if your 401(k) options are limited)

Coming Up . . .

We'll take a look at the Roth IRA, which flips the tax benefits around and gives you tax-free withdrawals instead of tax-deductible contributions. Spoiler: It's a favorite for younger investors and those expecting higher taxes later in life.

Roth IRA - Baker's Choice!

A Roth IRA is an individual retirement account that flips the traditional IRA on its head:

- No upfront tax deduction
- But 100% tax-free withdrawals in retirement

You contribute with after-tax dollars, meaning you've already paid tax on that money. So when you retire and start taking money out—*both your contributions and your investment earnings come out tax-free* (if you follow the rules).

2025 Roth IRA Contribution Limits

- Under age 50: $7,000
- Age 50 or older: $8,000 (thanks to catch-up contributions)

But there's a catch: you must fall within income limits to contribute directly to a Roth IRA. These limits are based on Modified Adjusted Gross Income (MAGI) and change each year.[15]

Roth Contribution Eligibility (2025)	Single	Married filing jointly
Full Contribution	Under $150,000	Under $236,000
Partial Contribution	$150,000	$236,000
Not Eligible	$165,000	$246,000

What If You Make Too Much to Qualify for a Roth IRA? Enter the *Backdoor* Roth IRA

High income earner? No problem. You may be able to use a legal work-around called the Backdoor Roth IRA.

This isn't a special type of account—it's just a strategy:

1. Contribute to a non-deductible traditional IRA
2. Convert that account to a Roth IRA

Yes, it's totally allowed. No, it's not shady. But it can trigger taxes, so . . .

> **BAKER'S CAVEAT:** Always work with a tax professional on a backdoor Roth. The rules are complex, and Uncle Sam still wants his cut—if you don't do it right.

Why Baker Loves the Roth IRA

Let's meet our guy Boo-Ray Boudreaux from Louisiana (because where else?). He's 25, just graduated from LSU in *gator husbandry*, and he's got a good head on his shoulders—and a Roth IRA.

---

15. Chart Source: Darrow Wealth Management, Boston, MA, https://darrowwealthmanagement.com/blog
/2025-contribution-limits-tax-brackets/

Scenario 1: Contributes $5,000/year for only 10 years

- From age 25–35
- Stops contributing entirely after age 35
- Investment return: 8%

By age 60, Boo-Ray would have $496,056—all TAX FREE.
Yes, just 10 years of saving turned into nearly half a million bucks.

Scenario 2: Contributes $5,000/year from age 25-60 (35 years total)

- Total contributions: $175,000
- Final account balance: $861,584 — TAX-FREE

Boo-Ray's Roth IRA Breakdown Breakdown

Contribution Summary	Amount
10 years x $5,000/year	$50,000
Investment earnings at 8%	$22,500 (by age 35)
Total after 10 years	$72,500

Contributions: You can withdraw these any time, tax and penalty-free.
Earnings: Hands off until age 59½, unless you want penalties.

That's right: Your Roth IRA can double as a back-up emergency fund, since your contributions are always accessible (but hopefully left alone to grow).

Why Roth IRAs Are Especially Powerful for Young Investors

- ✓ You're likely in a lower tax bracket now than you will be in retirement
- ✓ You have decades of compounding ahead of you
- ✓ You're locking in tax-free money for your future

Recap: Why Roth IRAs Rock[16]

✓ Contributions are after-tax.
✓ Earnings grow tax-free.
✓ Withdrawals in retirement are 100% tax-free.
✓ You can access your contributions anytime.
✓ Great for younger savers and those expecting higher future tax rates.

Make Your Children Roth IRA Millionaires

Want to give your kids a head start that could literally make them millionaires by retirement?

Say hello to one of the most underrated financial gifts out there: The Roth IRA for kids.

That's right! Minors are eligible to open a Roth IRA, provided they have earned income from a job or other qualifying work. That includes things like:

• Babysitting
• Lawn mowing
• Acting or modeling gigs
• Working in the family business (paid fairly)

Example: Make Cutie Suzi a Millionaire

Does cutie Suzi have earned income? Babysitting, mowing lawns . . .

Suzi has a babysitting job at age 12, earns $2,000 a year, and places it in a Custodial Roth IRA. Assuming an 8% return in her Roth IRA, in 6 years Suzi would have ~$14,672. She could withdraw $12,000 tax free and penalty free to pay toward her college tuition.

OR—If Suzi gets a full scholarship ride in college and continues $2,000/year into her Custodial Roth IRA until age 60, she would have ~$980,264 tax free at age 60.

Now, Suzi is a Golden Girl!

Let that sink in. Suzi becomes a Roth IRA millionaire by retirement, all because she started early, invested consistently, and let time and compound growth do their thing.

---

16. Calculations were made (of course) with the one and only Texas Instruments BA-35 calculator.

- ✓ Time is your child's biggest asset.
- ✓ Tax-free growth for decades is a superpower.
- ✓ Contributions can be withdrawn anytime, giving flexibility for emergencies or major milestones.

> **BAKER'S TIP:** You can gift your child the Roth IRA contributions (as long as they earned the money), making this a great combo gift: financial literacy + a future safety net.

Final Thought

If you want to give your kids the gift of financial independence, it doesn't get much better than this.

Start a Roth IRA while they're still young and working, even part time. You'll be planting seeds that could blossom into a seven-figure future.

How Do I Choose the Right Investments for My Retirement Plans?

Disclaimer: This is not investment or tax advice. It's meant to educate and empower you to have better conversations with your financial professional(s). You're the boss of your money!

Picture This . . .

Imagine your retirement plan as a big empty truck. It's your job to decide what to load into it.

If you have an employer-sponsored retirement plan (like a 401[k]), your truck comes with a pre-selected menu of maybe 20–35 investment options, usually mutual funds and ETFs. These may include:

- Large-cap US stock funds
- Small-cap stock funds
- International stock funds
- Government and corporate bond funds
- Target-date funds

At the very least, contribute enough to get your full employer match—it's free money!

With an individual retirement account (like a Roth IRA), the world is your warehouse. You can choose from thousands of investment options. The challenge, and the opportunity, is finding the right fit for you.

Investment Options to Consider

Your choices should depend on your:

- **Risk tolerance:** Does your temperament allow for the swings in the market?
- **Time horizon:** At what point will you need to take withdrawals (e.g., retirement age)?
- **Savings goals:** What are you saving money for (e.g., retirement)?
- **Personal values:** Do you want to invest in funds that meet your social stances and religious beliefs? See ESG investing later in this chapter.

Here are a few core investment styles and fund types to consider:

Target-Date Funds   Baker's Choice!

Target-date funds are the autopilot of retirement investing. These funds automatically adjust the balance of stocks, bonds, and cash equivalents based on your expected retirement year.

Example: If you're 25 years old in 2025 and plan to retire at age 60, you'd choose a 2060 Target-Date Fund. These funds are designed to start out aggressively, mostly invested in stocks, and then gradually become more conservative, shifting toward bonds and cash equivalents as your retirement date approaches. The chart below shows this shift.[17]

---

17. Chart source: https://www.empower.com/learning_center/investing/target-date-funds.shtml#/

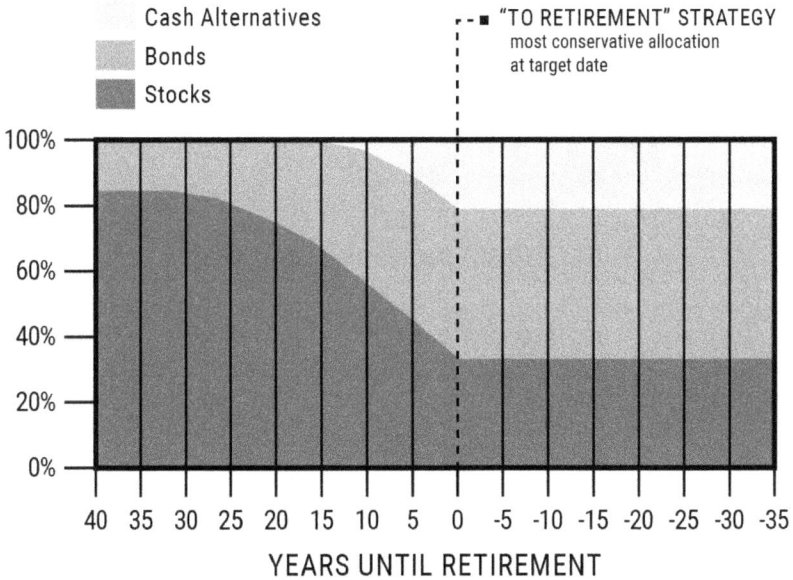

Legend:
- Cash Alternatives
- Bonds
- Stocks

"TO RETIREMENT" STRATEGY
most conservative allocation
at target date

Y-axis: 100%, 80%, 60%, 40%, 20%, 0%

X-axis: 40 35 30 25 20 15 10 5 0 -5 -10 -15 -20 -25 -30 -35

YEARS UNTIL RETIREMENT

Want more control? You can always choose a fund that targets an earlier or later year to reflect your risk preference.

Nearly every employer plan offers target-date funds, and they're a great one-stop option for investors who want simplicity.

Index Funds and ETFs   Baker's Choice! (Again!)

Index funds and ETFs aim to match the market, not beat it. They track indexes like the S&P 500 or the Total US Stock Market.

These funds are:

- Low-cost
- Diversified
- Proven performers over time

Fun fact: In 2024, only a very small percentage of fund managers have been able to outperform the S&P 500. Specifically, only 18.2% of actively managed funds outperformed the S&P 500 in the first half of 2024. Over the past decade, the average percentage of actively managed funds beating the S&P 500 has been even lower, at 27.1%. This suggests that the vast majority of fund managers struggle to consistently beat the market.[18]

If your plan has an S&P 500 index fund, it's a great foundation for your portfolio. The S&P 500 Index has returned an average of 12.06% in the past 45 years.[19]

The S&P 500 Performance Since 1980

1980: 25.77%	1989: 27.2%	1998: 26.67%	2007: 3.53%	2016: 9.54%
1981: **-9.73%**	1990: **-6.56%**	1999: 19.53%	2008: **-38.49%**	2017: 19.42%
1982: 14.76%	1991: 26.31%	2000: **-10.14%**	2009: 23.45%	2018: **-6.24%**
1983: 17.27%	1992: 4.45%	2001: **-13.04%**	2010: 12.78%	2019: 28.88%
1984: 1.40%	1993: 7.06%	2002: **-23.37%**	2011: 0.08%	2020: 16.26%
1985: 26.33%	1994: **-1.54%**	2003: 26.38%	2012: 13.41%	2021: 26.89%
1986: 14.62%	1995: 34.11%	2004: 8.99%	2013: 29.60%	2022: **-19.95%**
1987: 2.03%	1996: 20.26%	2005: 3.00%	2014: 11.39%	2023: 24.23%
1988: 12.40%	1997: 31.01%	2006: 13.62%	2015: **-0.73%**	2024: 25.89%

ESG Funds (Environmental, Social, Governance)
Baker Daughter's Choice!

If you're a values-driven investor, ESG funds might be for you. These funds screen investments based on things like:

- Sustainability
- Diversity and inclusion
- Ethical governance
- Social impact

Why it matters: Millennials and Gen Z are demanding more transparency and purpose from companies, and they're backing it up with their dollars.

A Morningstar study found 70% of Americans have at least a moderate interest in ESG investing.[20] A Natixis survey showed 71% of

---

18. Jason Zweig, "Why Your Fund Manager Can't Beat Today's Stock Market," *Wall Street Journal*, July 5, 2024, https://www.wsj.com/finance/investing/why-your-fund-manager-cant-beat-todays-stock-market-a5a14688.

19. Chart source: https://www.macrotrends.net/2324/sp-500-historical-chart-data

20. Morningstar, How Financial Advisors Use ESG Data to Build Portfolios, updated April 2025, accessed September 8, 2025, https://www.morningstar.com/views/blog/esg/portfolio-construction-for-financial-advisors.

Millennials would increase 401(k) contributions if their investments supported social good.[21]

A very small percentage of employer-sponsored retirement plans offer ESG (Environmental, Social, and Governance) investment options. According to surveys by the Plan Sponsor Council of America, only about 6.2% of defined contribution plans offered at least one ESG fund in 2023.[22]

Even if your 401(k) doesn't offer ESG funds, you can absolutely include them in your IRA or other self-directed accounts.

Religious-Based Mutual Funds
Your Faith-Based Choice

Faith-based investing is all about aligning your money with your values. These funds avoid companies and industries that conflict with religious beliefs and prioritize those that promote ethical principles.

Examples

- **Islamic Funds:** Like the *Iman Fund*, which avoids industries such as gambling, alcohol, pork, and interest-based finance.[23]
- **Christian Funds:** Like *Eventide Gilead*,[24] *Timothy Plan*,[25] and *Kingdom Impact Investing*,[26] focused on biblically responsible investing.
- **Catholic Funds:** *Ave Maria Mutual Funds27* and *Dana Epiphany ESG Equity Fund*.[28] Both funds are "Catholic-friendly," but Ave Maria sticks strictly to Roman Catholic values, investing only in companies that match those teachings, while Dana Epiphany is a

21. Arina Abbott, "How to Boost Millennial 401k Participation Rates," *401k Specialist,* March 22, 2017, https://401kspecialistmag.com/boost-millennial-401k-participation-rates.
22. Robert Steyer, "ESG funds haven't gained much traction in 401(k) plans or with DC plan consultants," *Pensions & Investments,* January 30, 2025, https://www.pionline.com/defined-contribution/esg-funds -havent-gained-much-traction-401k-plans-or-dc-plan-consultants#.
23. Allied Asset Advisors, *Home – Halal Investing with Iman Fund,* https://investaaa.com/.
24. Eventide Asset Management, *Mutual Funds Overview,* https://www.eventideinvestments.com/mutual-funds.
25. Timothy Plan, *Biblically Responsible Investing for Over 25 Years,* https://www.timothyplan.com.
26. Faith Driven Investor, *Investing for Kingdom Impact,* https://www.faithdriveninvestor.org/blog/investing -for-kingdom-impact.
27. Ave Maria Mutual Funds, *Biblically Responsible Investing with Catholic Values,* https://avemariafunds.com.
28. Dana Investment Advisors, *Epiphany ESG Equity Fund Market Commentary: Overview,* https://www.danafunds .com/commentaries/epiphany-esg-equity-fund-market-commentary/overview/.

bit broader, using Catholic guidelines to help pick companies, but not limiting themselves to just Catholic investments.

- **Denomination-Specific Funds:** *Praxis Mutual Funds* (Mennonite),[29] *New Covenant Funds* (Presbyterian),[30] and more, which focus on principles and values of different denominations and often have elements of charitable giving.

This is your chance to let your values lead your investing, while still pursuing long-term growth.

Final Thoughts

Choosing investments doesn't have to be overwhelming. Start with your goals, match them with your values and risk tolerance, and then pick options that align. Whether you're all about simplicity, low fees, values, or growth, there's a fund (or mix of funds) for you.

There is an old adage, "It's not about timing the stock market, but about time in the stock market," that has proven true again and again. People who stay invested in a well-diversified portfolio over the long run almost always come out ahead of those who try to chase market highs and lows.[31]

HIRING A FINANCIAL PLANNER: WHO CAN YOU TRUST WITH YOUR FUTURE?

One of the most common questions I get is: "Should I hire a financial planner?"

The answer? Maybe.

Whether you DIY or work with a pro, this book is here to help you become an *informed* and *empowered* investor. But if you do choose to hire someone, I want to make sure you know what to look for and what to avoid.

---

29. Praxis Mutual Funds, *Investing Together, Impacting the World*, https://www.praxisinvests.com.

30. New Covenant Funds, *Socially Responsible Investing with Presbyterian Values*, https://www.newcovenantfunds.com.

31. Alexandra Nortier, "Time in the market vs timing the market?", *Investec*, August 11, 2025, https://www.investec.com/en_za/focus/investing/why-it-doesnt-pay-to-time-the-market.html.

What Is a Financial Planner, Really?

"Financial planner" isn't a regulated title. Anyone can slap it on a business card, even someone who's really just an insurance salesperson.

That's why you need to look beyond the job title and dig into credentials, compensation, and ethics.

Baker's Checklist for Hiring a Financial Planner

○ They Must Be a Fiduciary.

This is non-negotiable.

A fiduciary is legally and ethically required to act in your best interest at all times. That might sound like a given, but it's not. Many "advisors" operate under a looser standard that only requires advice to be "suitable," not necessarily best for you.

According to the Council of Economic Advisers, Americans lose an estimated *$17 billion per year* due to conflicted financial advice.[32]

So always ask: "Are you a fiduciary, 100% of the time?"

○ Hire a Fee-Only Advisor (Not Fee-Based).

Fee-only planners are paid only by you. They don't receive commissions from selling financial products, so they have far fewer conflicts of interest.

Avoid:

- ✗ Commission-based advisors (paid to sell)
- ✗ Fee-based advisors (paid by both you *and* commissions)

○ Look for the CFP® Credential.

A Certified Financial Planner™ (CFP®) has met strict educational, ethical, and experience requirements. They're trained to help you with:

- Retirement planning
- College savings
- Debt reduction

---

32. U.S. Department of Labor, *White House Fact Sheet: Strengthening Retirement Security by Cracking Down on Conflicts of Interest in Retirement Savings*, news release, April 6, 2016, accessed September 8, 2025, https://www.dol.gov/newsroom/releases/ebsa/ebsa20160406-0.

- Estate planning
- Investment strategy
- And more

To become a CFP®, someone must:

- Complete 4,000+ hours of experience
- Pass a rigorous exam
- Commit to ongoing education and a strict code of ethics

⭕ Do Your Homework: Run a Broker Check.

Before you hire anyone, check their background. Use FINRA's BrokerCheck to find out:[33]

- Are they licensed?
- Have they ever been investigated?
- Any disciplinary actions or complaints?

Or call FINRA at 800-289-9999.

⭕ Ask These 6 Questions Before You Hire Anyone.

1. Are you and your firm registered with FINRA or the SEC?
2. Are you a fiduciary at all times?
3. How are you paid—commission, flat fee, or percentage of assets?
4. Have you ever been convicted or charged with a crime?
5. Has any regulatory agency ever investigated you?
6. Will you provide all fees in writing?

Yes, even ask your cousin, your best friend, or your dad's golf buddy. If they're legit, they won't be offended.

---

33. Financial Industry Regulatory Authority (FINRA), *BrokerCheck*, https://brokercheck.finra.org.

Baker's Choice!

If you don't have someone in mind, look for a planner who is:

- Fee-only
- A fiduciary
- CFP® certified
- Transparent and unconflicted

Don't rush the process. You're not just hiring someone to manage money—you're hiring someone to guide your future.

I personally know of a securities broker who cycled through four different brokerage firms in just nine years. At each stop, he faced disciplinary action, both from his employer and from FINRA. His record on FINRA's BrokerCheck page reads like a warning label. Here are just a few of the official complaints:

- Customer Dispute: Alleged unsuitable investments
- Customer Dispute: Fraudulent representations and falsified account agreements
- Financial: Bankruptcy
- Customer Dispute: Unauthorized trades
- Customer Dispute: Unauthorized trades and breach of fiduciary duty
- Customer Dispute: Unsuitable investments
- Customer Dispute: Unauthorized trades

And to top it off, he's currently employed at yet another brokerage firm, thanks to a family connection. It raises a fair question: why didn't his previous employers do their due diligence before hiring him?

The lesson here is clear: you must do your own homework. Before doing business with any financial advisor, take the time to research their background. Tools like FINRA's BrokerCheck exist for a reason, so use them.

And remember: A bad advisor can cost you way more than just fees. Due diligence upfront could save you from major regrets, or an unexpected trip to Madagascar (See: Principle #11: Protect Your ASSets From Investment Fraud).

ALTERNATIVE INVESTMENTS: BEYOND STOCKS AND BONDS

Let's step off the beaten path for a moment.

Most of this book focuses on foundational investments—stocks, bonds, and cash equivalents—because they're time-tested, well-regulated, and ideal for long-term growth.

But what about alternative investments?

Alternative investments fall outside the conventional categories and can include:

- Real estate
- Commodities
- Hedge funds
- Cryptocurrencies
- Private equity
- Collectibles (art, wine, watches, etc.)

Some of these may eventually play a role in your portfolio, but they're not for everyone. For most people, I recommend building a strong financial base first. But it's still smart to know what else is out there.

Let's explore one of the most common, and accessible, alternatives: real estate.

Investing in Real Estate (Rental Properties)

I've known plenty of people who've built wealth through real estate, especially rental properties. But make no mistake, this isn't a set-it-and-forget-it investment like a mutual fund. It takes homework, hustle, and a willingness to get your hands dirty (sometimes literally).

Since I've never owned a rental property myself, I turned to Blake Johnson, a former student and pharmacist who's walked the walk.

Turning Real Estate into a Wealth Engine

Blake Johnson graduated from pharmacy school in 2013 with a solid plan: pay off his student loans, max out his 401(k), and then figure out how to grow his wealth. When pharmacist raises started to plateau, Blake began looking for new ways to boost his income.

That's when he discovered real estate and a business partner with remodeling skills. In 2018, they bought their first rental property. Fast forward to 2025, and the duo now co-own ~50 properties, with minimal out-of-pocket investment. Not too shabby for someone in their mid-30s!

Here's what Blake shared about the real pros and cons of rental property investing:

Advantages:

- Tenants pay your mortgage, building equity every month.
- Properties typically appreciate over time, like stocks.
- Tax perks: depreciation, mortgage interest, repairs, and more.
- Full control of your investment—flexible and customizable.
- Unlike a 401(k), you can access profits before retirement.
- Partnerships can reduce your workload and capital requirements.
- Passive income can eventually replace your salary.
- Diversification: residential, multi-family, and commercial options.
- Leverage: use the bank's money to amplify returns.
- Multiple exit strategies—rent, sell, trade, or even live in it.

Disadvantages:

- It's not truly passive—expect sweat equity and tenant headaches.
- Vacancies still mean mortgage payments.
- Legal and liability risks are real.
- Managing tenants can be time-consuming (and draining).
- Real estate isn't liquid—quick access to cash isn't guaranteed.
- Ongoing costs: insurance, repairs, taxes, and maintenance.
- Market risk—home values rise and fall.

Bottom line: Real estate can be a powerful path to financial freedom, but it's no walk in the park. Blake's success didn't come by accident. It took planning, partnership, and a willingness to treat real estate like a real business.

Real Estate Investment Trusts (REITs)

Want real estate exposure *without* the hassle of managing tenants or toilets?

Enter the REIT—Real Estate Investment Trust.

A REIT is a company that owns and operates income-producing real estate. When you invest in a REIT, you're essentially buying shares of that company, just like you would a mutual fund.

REITs:

- Trade on the stock market
- Are easy to buy and sell
- Offer dividend income
- Require little capital to start

They invest in everything from apartments to office buildings, shopping malls, data centers, and even cell towers. And just like mutual funds, they offer diversification, except in real estate instead of stocks.

Final Word on Alternatives

Alternative investments can diversify your portfolio and generate income, but they come with complexity and risk. For most people, they're best approached *after* you've built a strong foundation in traditional investments. In other words: Don't skip dinner to go straight to dessert.

Warren Buffet once said, *"Never invest in a business you cannot understand."*

Back in 2013, a tech-savvy friend in California introduced me to something new and intriguing: cryptocurrency—specifically, Bitcoin. I did some research and was drawn in by the potential for explosive gains (and equally explosive risk). As an early adopter and curious investor, I dipped my toes in.

Buying Bitcoin back then wasn't easy. The most prominent exchange, Mt. Gox handled nearly 80% of all BTC transactions. It also had a reputation for being difficult to use—and vulnerable to hacks. Still, I pressed on.

After weeks of account verification, I started buying Bitcoin the only way I could: four $500 money orders from Walmart, sent to a company I barely trusted, referencing a long string of random wallet code. Honestly, I wasn't even sure it was legal.

Eventually, my wallet showed 20 Bitcoin. I was in the game! But with each rise in value came news of another exchange getting hacked. Then came the bombshell: in 2014, Mt. Gox was exposed for losing 750,000 BTC—worth nearly half a billion dollars. I panicked and sold everything for a small profit.

Fast forward to 2017 . . . Bitcoin hit $20,000. My former 20 BTC? Worth around $400,000.

Moral of the story: I got in early, got out scared, and paid the price in hindsight. It was a $400,000 lesson in risk, timing, and conviction.

"Success in investing doesn't correlate with IQ . . . what you need is the temperament to control the urges that get other people into trouble in investing"

Warren Buffett

PRINCIPLE #9

Don't Get Hustled

"If it sounds too good to be true, it probably is."

It often starts with a text from someone you haven't talked to in a while.

"Hey! I've been thinking about you! How's everything going? I've got something exciting I'd love to share . . . "

Sometimes it's a Facebook post showing off a new car, a weekend retreat, or the promise of "working from anywhere." Other times, it's an innocent-looking party invite, with wine and appetizers and . . . a whiteboard waiting in the corner.

They call it *an opportunity*. A chance to be your own boss. To build wealth on your own terms. To finally break free from your job, your debt, your stress.

It sounds amazing. It feels empowering. And it's almost always sold by someone you know and trust.

That's what makes this chapter one of the most important in the book.

Because these offers—whether they come dressed up as side hustles, timeshares, miracle investments, or game-changing "businesses"—don't just cost people money. They cost relationships. Time. Trust. And for many, they cost years of financial progress.

I've been pitched. I've bought in. I've lost. And now I want to make sure you don't have to learn the hard way like I did.

Let's break down why these promises are so dangerous and how to protect yourself from the financial predators hiding behind inspirational hashtags and shiny opportunity decks.

WHY THESE PITCHES WORK

The psychology behind multilevel marketing schemes is powerful. They:

- Appeal to your desire for quick fixes
- Offer emotional stories of rags-to-riches success
- Promise community and belonging
- Prey on your financial stress or student debt

Worst of all, these offers often come from people you know like a friend, cousin, or former classmate who truly believes what they're selling.

And that's what makes it so hard to say no.

Red Flags to Watch For

Here's a cheat sheet for spotting a sketchy scheme:

- ✘ Emphasis on recruiting others rather than selling an actual product
- ✘ Confusing compensation plans with lots of "upline/downline" jargon
- ✘ High starter kit fees or recurring membership costs
- ✘ Promises of "passive income" for minimal effort
- ✘ Emotional rags-to-riches stories with no financial transparency
- ✘ Vague or overpriced products, often hard to sell outside the system
- ✘ Pushy sales tactics disguised as casual conversations or "opportunities"

A Real-Life Conversation

While I was writing this chapter, I got a Facebook message from someone I'd never met, but we had a bunch of mutual friends. Here's how it went:

Ms. MLM: "Hey, Joey! Would you be open to a side project that doesn't interfere with your current work?"
Me: "What kind of project?"

Ms. MLM: "It's a global opportunity to help others reach their dreams! Let me send you a video . . . "
Me: "I'm not comfortable with MLMs, but I wish you all the best."
Ms. MLM: "What makes you uncomfortable?"
Me: "I'm leery of companies that focus on recruiting over product quality, and ones that require membership fees to earn money."

Sometimes the kindest thing you can do, for both yourself and them, is just to be honest.

The Stats Don't Lie

Can you make money in MLMs? Technically, yes. But the odds are stacked high against you.

- A 2020 AARP study found that 73% of participants in MLMs either lost money or made nothing at all.[1]
- Other consumer advocacy reports estimate that 99% of participants fail to earn a profit, with most income flowing to those at the very top.[2]
- Costs like membership fees, starter kits, training seminars, and travel often wipe out any potential gains.

"Profit" isn't just money coming in; it's what's left after your expenses. And most people walk away in the red.

The line between MLMs and pyramid schemes is often blurred. People will often say, "It's legal, so it can't be a pyramid scheme, right?"

Not necessarily.

The Federal Trade Commission (FTC) has investigated multilevel marketing companies for years. If a business makes most of its money from recruiting rather than selling products to consumers, it may cross the legal line into pyramid scheme territory, even if it hasn't been shut down yet.

1. Jean Chatzky, "Advice for Job Seekers Tempted by Multilevel Marketing Offers," *AARP*, August 13, 2020, https://www.aarp.org/work/job-search/advice-for-job-seekers-tempted-by-multilevel-marketing-offers.
2. Jon M. Taylor, *Chapter 7: MLM's Abysmal Numbers – The Case (for and) Against Multi-Level Marketing*, Consumer Awareness Institute, public comment submitted to the Federal Trade Commission, April 6, 2016, accessed September 8, 2025, https://www.ftc.gov/sites/default/files/documents/public_comments/trade-regulation-rule-disclosure-requirements-and-prohibitions-concerning-business-opportunities-ftc.r511993-00008%C2%A0/00008-57281.pdf.

How to Say No (Without the Guilt)

It's okay to say no to MLMs, schemes, and pressure from people you care about. Try one of these:

- "Thanks for thinking of me, but this isn't a good fit for where I'm at financially."
- "I'd rather support you as a friend than be part of the business."
- "I've done the research, and I'm not comfortable joining."

BAKER'S STORY: MY EARLY MLM LESSON

Just after college in the late 1970s, I was invited to my old econ professor's house for a "business opportunity." He started drawing big circles on a blackboard and pitched us on selling *Amway*.[3]

It wasn't about the products, but more about enlisting others. I spent time, energy, and money. I believed. I failed.

It wouldn't be my last run-in with multilevel marketing. But it taught me a lesson that's now baked into this book:

"Those who cannot remember the past
are condemned to repeat it."

George Santayana

---

3. Amway is an American multilevel marketing company that sells health, beauty, and home care products. The company was founded in 1959 and was one of the first multilevel marketing companies. See www .amway.com.

BETTER ALTERNATIVES TO MAKE MONEY

Instead of joining a scheme, consider:

- ✓ Freelancing a skill you already have
- ✓ Starting a side hustle (writing, design, tutoring, AI)
- ✓ Investing in dividend stocks or REITs
- ✓ Building a business with a real product or service

Entrepreneurship is great. But it shouldn't come with pressure, deception, or debt. "Would I still do this if I had to sell the product, but could never recruit a single person?"

If the answer is no, walk away.

Pyramid Schemes

Pyramid schemes often resemble multilevel marketing (MLM) companies in structure, but there's one key difference—they're illegal investment scams. These schemes rely on a constant stream of new recruits whose money funds the promised "returns" for earlier participants. There's no actual investment, just a redistribution of incoming funds.

The model works by offering guaranteed high returns to entice new investors. At first, early participants do see impressive payouts, but those gains are entirely funded by money from new recruits. Eventually, when new recruits dry up, the entire system collapses.

One of the most infamous examples is Bernie Madoff, a once-respected financier who orchestrated the largest Ponzi scheme in history. Over 17 years, he defrauded thousands of investors out of billions of dollars, all by using new investors' money to pay off earlier ones. In 2009, Madoff pleaded guilty to 11 felony counts and was sentenced to 150 years in prison. His story serves as a powerful warning: if returns are guaranteed and sound too good to be true, then they probably are.

I was once talked into attending a late-night hotel meeting. That alone should've been a red flag because nothing good starts with, "Just meet me at the Marriott conference room after dark."

The pitch came from a "friend" who told me it was a legit opportunity to sell insurance. I raised an eyebrow and said, "You know this sounds like a pyramid scheme, right?" He got defensive—like, vein-popping, "I-thought-we-were-brothers" defensive. But I agreed to go . . . because, hey, friendship.

When I arrived, everyone greeted me with unsettling enthusiasm—a kind of "drink this Kool-Aid and unlock your dreams" vibe.[4] The presenter dimmed the lights and fired up the PowerPoint. First slide: their company logo . . . shaped like a pyramid. I looked over at my friend, who now couldn't make eye contact.

Slide two broke the pyramid into tiers. Slide three never came, because that's when I decided to slip quietly out the back door like someone dodging a cult initiation.

Later, I did some digging. Turns out, this wasn't about selling insurance at all; it was about getting people to sign others up to maybe sell insurance. No one actually sold anything except the dream and a $199 "starter kit."

Timeshares

Yes, the rumors are true—my wife and I spent part of our honeymoon at a timeshare presentation. (See Baker's Dirty Dozen Principle #2: Make sure your significant other shares your financial goals.)

It was 1985. We were broke but in love and determined to get out of town. Instead of charging a tropical getaway to a credit card, we found a deal we couldn't resist: a free 3-day, 2-night stay at Fairfield Bay in Northern Arkansas. Sure, it was a retirement community—but hey, it was peaceful, came with a couple of free meals, and included a round of golf with a cart!

---

4. "When someone tells you *don't drink the Kool-Aid*, they mean to not get taken in by anything, an idea, a fashion, or a person, to the extent that you dedicate your very existence to it. It means, especially, to avoid any groups who seem fanatical in their beliefs." (CulinaryLore, *Why Do People Say "Don't Drink the Kool-Aid?"*, updated July 10, 2025, https://culinarylore.com/food-history:why-do-people-say-dont-drink-the-kool-aid.)

And let's be honest, if you're doing your honeymoon right, it doesn't matter if you're in Mexico or a Motel 6. We figured, why not get a vacation and a sales pitch all in one?

Since then, we've attended over a dozen timeshare presentations and, proudly, never bought a single one. Why do we keep going? Because two hours of listening to a high-pressure sales rep with slick hair and big promises is a small price to pay for free hotel stays, restaurant coupons, or yes, more golf.

> **BAKER'S TIP:** If you can nod politely and say, "We'll think about it" for 120 minutes straight, you too can enjoy the finer things in life . . . without ever owning a single week in Orlando.

What's a Timeshare (and Why You Probably Don't Want One)

A timeshare is a property arrangement where multiple people share the right to use the same property—usually for vacation purposes—during specific times of the year. This can include condos, homes, resorts, and yes, even luxury RVs, yachts, and private jets (because nothing says "smart investment" like co-owning a boat you never drive).

Baker's Nitty-Gritty on Timeshares

Let's be clear: buying a timeshare is not an investment. Even the Federal Trade Commission (FTC) spells this out plainly: "The value of these options is in their use as vacation destinations, not as investments." Translation? You're paying for the privilege to vacation, not to build wealth.

And that privilege isn't cheap. Timeshares often come with a hefty upfront cost—one that depreciates faster than a car driven off the lot. On top of that, you'll typically face:

- ✘ High-interest loan payments (if financed)
- ✘ Annual maintenance fees that tend to rise like your blood pressure when they arrive
- ✘ Limited flexibility on when and where you can vacation
- ✘ A resale market that's about as lively as a Blockbuster Video

To make matters worse, selling a timeshare can be like trying to get rid of a haunted treadmill—nobody wants it, and it just keeps showing up.

Look, I've met very few people who've said, "Buying a timeshare was one of my best financial decisions!" Most have the same story: it sounded like a deal . . . until it wasn't.

So, unless you're a professional negotiator with a passion for prepaid vacations and recurring fees, think long and hard before signing on that dotted line. I don't recommend it.

For more info (and a dose of government-backed reality), check out: Timeshares and Vacation Plans | FTC.[5]

ROBERT EDGIN: What I Wish I'd Known Sooner

I'm a retired pharmacist, and if I'm honest, I made a few financial decisions I wish I could take back, especially the two timeshares I bought 15–20 years ago. One of them I never used, not once. The other, maybe three or four times in two decades. Yet I kept paying the $400–$500 annual maintenance fees like clockwork. Looking back, those purchases felt like a good idea at the time, but they turned into money pits. If I had known then what I know now, and followed the principles in this book, I'd be debt-free today at 73.[6]

Gambling

Gambling can spiral out of control before you realize what's happening. That rush from a big win? It can blind you to the fact that, over time, you're almost always losing more than you're winning. Unless you're Matt Damon playing poker in *Rounders*, you're probably better off watching the World Series of Poker from your recliner with your wallet safely across the room.

Gambling takes many forms: casinos, sports betting, scratch-offs, and the ever-elusive lottery. We've all imagined winning big and retiring early. In 2018, the Powerball jackpot hit $550 million, yet no one won after multiple drawings. The odds? About 1 in 292 million. But that doesn't stop people from throwing money at the dream.[7] The average person spends

---

5. Federal Trade Commission, *Timeshares, Vacation Clubs, and Related Scams*, updated July 10, 2025, https://consumer.ftc.gov/articles/timeshares-vacation-clubs-and-related-scams.
6. This is a snippet from an Amazon Review of the first edition of *Baker's Dirty Dozen*.
7. Michael E. Ruane, "There's Still a Chance: Two Big Lotteries Still Have No Winners," *Washington Post*, January 5, 2018, https://www.washingtonpost.com/news/local/wp/2018/01/05/theres-still-a-chance-two-big-lotteries-still-have-no-winners.

about $1,038 a year on lottery tickets for a chance at disappointment and a trash can full of losing tickets.[8]

Full disclosure: I've played the Powerball, but less than five times. But only for "defensive" purposes. When my card-playing buddies pooled money for tickets, I joined in. If they hit the jackpot, I didn't want to be the guy still working on Monday. Plus, let's face it—someone's gotta be the financial planner in the group.

If you think you, or someone you know, may have a gambling problem, don't ignore it. The National Problem Gambling Helpline is available 24/7: 1-800-522-4700.[9]

Remember:

> "It's not how much you make,
> but how much you keep."
>
> **Robert Kiyosaki**

SHANE T. LESTER: Gambling: The House Always Wins

Gambling has been in my life as far back as I can remember. My dad thought he could make a living from it after being laid off, and one night my mom told him not to come home without the rent money. The next call we got was from the police, in which he had been arrested for multiple robberies. Though it was his first offense, he received four 20-year sentences (served four years with good behavior) and spent the rest of his life trying to make it up to me and my mom.

Years later, I stopped in Tunica on the way to a golf trip, won $700 at roulette, and before the casino returned our licenses, I'd lost $4,500. I didn't even have a debit card. I had to call a buddy to wire us cash to finish the trip. Then in Vegas, my wife played $3 hands, thrilled by $10 wins, while I quietly lost $7,000 betting hundreds a spin.

---

8. Megan Leonhardt, "Americans Spend Over $1,000 a Year on Lotto Tickets," *CNBC*, December 12, 2019, https://www.cnbc.com/2019/12/12/americans-spend-over-1000-dollars-a-year-on-lotto-tickets.htm. See also Sarah Foster, "Americans Spend Over $1,000 a Year on Lottery Tickets," *Bankrate*, September 2018, https://www.bankrate.com/personal-finance/smart-money/financial-vices-september-2018.

9. National Council on Problem Gambling, *About the National Problem Gambling Helpline*, accessed September 8, 2025, https://www.ncpgambling.org/help-treatment/about-the-national-problem-gambling-helpline/.

The wake-up call came in 2008 after I lost $20,000 betting on football in a single weekend. My wife, calmly and without judgment, asked, "How many times have you won?"

I smiled and said, "Well, you know I've won."

She paused, then clarified, "No, I mean *this year.*"

As I sat there trying to come up with an answer, she simply said, "Huh."

That little sound hit me harder than any loss I'd ever had. I haven't placed a bet on football since.

Baker's Dirty Dozen
PRINCIPLE #10

Buy the Right House and Pick the Right Mortgage

LEE BRENT, MBA: Welcome Home!

We were so proud when my daughter and son-in-law bought their house. They could not believe how many papers they had to sign at closing; they swore they developed carpal tunnel syndrome as a result.

About a week after they moved in, my daughter called and said, "Dad, snow blowers cost $400, lawn mowers are $350, weed whackers $150, and edger's are $125!" Wow, who knew? Did she think they came with the house? Over the next couple of weeks, we got similar phone calls bemoaning the cost of paint, a shop vacuum, and ceiling fans.

A couple of months before they decided on a house, I told them to get ready for an emotional roller coaster—buying a home is more painful than planning a wedding. In a sense, they were getting married to a house. Would the seller accept their offer? Would there be a counteroffer? Would the home appraise high enough for the loan? Would the inspection find structural damage? Radon? Water damage? Termites? Mold?

They are educated—my daughter is a PharmD (pharmacist) and my son-in-law is a school teacher with a degree in history and a minor in music. They had met with a realtor and a banker and were sure they were ready for whatever was coming. They had no idea they were entering the Twilight Zone of finance, insurance, and real estate.

Well before the close, I got them to combine their homeowner's insurance and their car insurance with one carrier. They were excited to get the discounts and better coverage, plus it was simple enough that no explanation was required. For a fleeting moment I was the cost savings guru—I was on a roll.

Then I stepped on the Private Mortgage Insurance (PMI) landmine. I told them that PMI generally costs 1% of the mortgage per year and would be about $3,500 annually until the equity in their home reached or exceeded 20% of the sales price.

The response I got was not unexpected.

They were incredulous. "We will be paying homeowner's insurance, mortgage insurance, title insurance, and what the hell is PMI?" Did you ever say something you knew would not be well received? I said, "It protects the lender if you can't pay your mortgage and your house goes into foreclosure." My daughter raised her voice and actually yelled, "We just signed our life away and we have to pay for the bank's insurance policy?"

I didn't realize I would be joining them on their homebuying rollercoaster ride. I decided to let someone else explain the rest of the closing costs, which would include flood determination, loan discount points, transfer taxes, lead-based paint inspection, application fee, and a half dozen more.

I did buy them a lawn mower!

BUYING A HOUSE—OH, WHAT FUN!

Ready to take the big leap into homeownership? Before you start picking out paint colors and practicing your lawn-mowing skills, ask yourself: Why are you buying a home? Is it the dream of finally having a place to call your own? Are you tired of paying rent that just helps your landlord pay their mortgage? Or maybe . . . it's time to move out of your parents' house (no shame—the "boomerang kid" era has been real). Either way, owning a home is exciting. But just remember, with great square footage comes great responsibility . . . and probably a leaky faucet.

Since buying a house is likely the single biggest financial purchase you'll ever make, it's crucial to slow down, think carefully, and buy for the right reasons, not just because it feels like "the next step."

Rent or Own—That Is the Question!

Buying a home can be a thrilling experience, but it can also be stressful, expensive, and at times downright confusing. The real question: Are you truly ready for everything that comes with owning a home?

It's easy to romanticize the idea of homeownership (Instagram-worthy kitchens! Backyard barbecues!), but it's important to go into it with eyes wide open.

Remember the 1986 movie *The Money Pit*, starring Tom Hanks and Shelley Long? It's billed as a comedy, but if you've ever watched it, you know it's more like a slow-motion horror show for new homeowners.

If you want a more current version, just spend five minutes on TikTok and you'll find thousands of videos showing first-time homeowners realizing they now have to fix leaking roofs, exploding water heaters, and mysterious basement smells, all without a landlord to call.

How Long Are You Planning to Stay?

If you're not planning to stick around for at least 3–5 years, it might make more financial sense to rent. Buying and selling homes comes with major costs including real estate commissions, moving expenses, and potential market dips that can eat into your investment if you move too soon.

Can I Really Afford a House Right Now?

It's not just about whether you *can* get approved for a mortgage; it's about whether you're truly ready for all the expenses that come with owning. Beyond your monthly mortgage payment, don't forget about:

- Homeowners insurance
- Property taxes
- Private mortgage insurance (if you put down less than 20%)
- Routine maintenance and repairs
- Emergency fixes (because your air conditioning *will* break during a heatwave)

A good rule of thumb: Budget 1–4% of the home's value each year for maintenance and unexpected repairs. Newer homes tend to cost less; older homes can surprise you with major expenses.[1]

Tools to Help You Decide

There are lots of free online calculators that can help you crunch the numbers:

- Bankrate Rent vs. Buy Calculator[2]
- Zillow's Affordability Calculator[3]
- NerdWallet Rent vs. Buy Calculator[4]

Don't just trust your gut—run the numbers.

BUYING A HOUSE

How Much House Can You Really Afford (Without Eating Ramen Every Night)?

One of the golden rules lenders use today is called the 28/36 Rule. It says:

- Your mortgage payment (principal, interest, taxes, and insurance— a.k.a. PITI) should not exceed 28% of your gross monthly income.
- All of your debt combined (car loans, student loans, credit cards, etc.) should not exceed 36% of your gross monthly income.[5]

Some financial experts, like Dave Ramsey, are even more conservative, recommending that no more than 25% of your *net* income goes toward your mortgage.

Where should you land? Somewhere between 25% of your *net* and 28% of your *gross*—depending on your lifestyle and financial goals.

1. Fannie Mae, *How to Build Your Maintenance and Repair Budget*, accessed September 9, 2025, https://yourhome .fanniemae.com/own/how-build-your-maintenance-and-repair-budget.
2. Bankrate, *Rent vs. Buy Calculator*, accessed September 9, 2025, https://www.bankrate.com/mortgages/rent -or-buy-home-calculator/.
3. Zillow, *Affordability Calculator – How Much House Can I Afford?*, accessed September 9, 2025, https://www .zillow.com/mortgage-calculator/house-affordability/.
4. NerdWallet, *Rent vs Buy Calculator*, written by Abby Badach Doyle and edited by Jeanette Margle, accessed September 9, 2025, https://www.nerdwallet.com/calculator/rent-vs-buy-calculator.
5. Julia Kagan, "28/36 Rule: What It Is, How to Use It, Example," *Investopedia*, last updated October 20, 2024, https://www.investopedia.com/terms/t/twenty-eight-thirty-six-rule.asp.

> **BAKER'S BOTTOM LINE:** Find a housing payment that fits *your* budget and not the lender's.[6]

Pre-Qualified vs. Pre-Approved: Flirting vs. Getting Engaged

Before you fall in love with a dream house, you need to know what you can actually afford. Here's the difference between pre-qualified and pre-approved:

- **Pre-Qualified:** A casual estimate based on information you provide about your income, debts, and assets. No deep dive. Can usually be done online or over the phone and is usually free.
- **Pre-Approved:** A full financial inspection. You'll fill out an official mortgage application, your credit will be pulled, and you'll provide pay stubs, tax returns, and proof of assets. Some lenders charge a small fee for this, but it gives you a real number you can bank on when you go to make an offer.

> **IMPORTANT:** Once you're pre-approved, DO NOT open any new credit cards, take out a car loan, or make big purchases until after your home closes. Trust me. Lenders watch that stuff like hawks.

Just Because You *Can* Doesn't Mean You *Should*

Remember: Mortgage lenders sell money. Just because they *say* you can afford a $500,000 home doesn't mean you should buy one. Stick to *your* budget.

---

6. David McMillin, *How Much House Can I Afford?*, Bankrate, last updated January 7, 2025, https://www .bankrate.com/real-estate/new-house-calculator/; Rachel Cruze, *How to Buy a Home in 2025*, Ramsey Solutions, July 30, 2025, https://www.ramseysolutions.com/real-estate/how-to-buy-a-house.

Bank or Broker: Who Should You Trust with Your Mortgage?

- **Mortgage Bank:** Offers loans only from their institution. Limited options but streamlined process.
- **Mortgage Broker:** Shops your loan across multiple lenders to find you the best deal. More choices, possibly better rates.

> **BAKER'S TIP:** Get quotes from both a bank and a broker. It doesn't hurt to compare.

Fixed, Adjustable, or Just Confused? Picking the Right Mortgage

Mortgages come in all flavors:

- **Fixed Rate Mortgage:** Same rate for 15, 20, or 30 years. Predictable and stable.
- **Adjustable Rate Mortgage (ARM):** Rate changes over time. Starts lower but can rise later.

> **BAKER'S CHOICE:** Strongly consider a 15-year or 20-year fixed mortgage if you can swing it. Use a calculator like NerdWallet's 15 vs. 30 Year Mortgage Tool to see the massive interest savings.[7]

A Quick Guide to Alphabet Soup Mortgages

There are multiple types of mortgages out there. A good lender can walk you through options like:

- Conventional loans (most common)
- FHA loans (easier qualification, smaller down payment)
- VA loans (for veterans and active-duty military)
- USDA loans (for rural properties)

---

7. Holden Lewis, *15-Year vs. 30-Year Mortgage Calculator*, NerdWallet, last updated April 25, 2025, https://www.nerdwallet.com/article/mortgages/15-or-30-year-mortgage-calculator.

Loans are always evolving, so make sure you get a fresh explanation before you choose.

PMI: The Sneaky Fee You'll Want to Dodge

Private Mortgage Insurance (PMI) protects the lender, not you. It kicks in if you put down less than 20%.

Current PMI costs range from 0.55% to 2.25% of your original loan amount per year.[8]

Putting down 20% saves you this extra cost and it adds up!

Do I Really Need a Realtor®? (Spoiler: Yes.)

Short answer: YES. And bonus: With the right negotiation and contract terms, it's possible for the seller to cover the buyer's agent commission.

A good buyer's agent will:

- Help you find listings that fit your needs
- Negotiate the best deal
- Guide you through inspections and repairs
- Keep the process moving smoothly through closing

It's like having a coach for the biggest financial game of your life.

House Hunting 101: Where to Start Swiping Right

Start browsing on websites like:

- Zillow
- Realtor.com—generally updates listings every 15 minutes
- Redfin

Online browsing helps you figure out neighborhoods, prices, and must-haves before you fall head over heels.

Appraisals, Title Searches, and Inspections—Oh My!

- **Appraisal:** Required by lenders. Ensures you're not wildly overpaying and protects the lenders.

---

8. Solarity Credit Union, *A PMI Primer: What Is Private Mortgage Insurance?*, accessed September 9, 2025, https://www.solaritycu.org/post/articles/a-pmi-primer-what-is-private-mortgage-insurance.

- **Title Search:** Finds any liens (debts) against the property.
- **Termite Inspections:** Required by some lenders, especially FHA and VA loans.

Title Insurance: Your Home's Secret Bodyguard

Title Insurance protects you if someone later claims ownership of your property. There are two policies:

- **Owner's Policy:** Protects *you* (Make sure you get this policy!)
- **Lender's Policy:** Protects your lender

Common title issues it protects against:

- Unpaid property taxes
- Mistakes in legal documents
- Unknown heirs showing up
- Hidden liens

One-time cost, lifelong peace of mind.

Home Inspections: Protect Your Wallet (and Your Sanity)

Spend the $300–$600 for a full home inspection by a licensed inspector. They'll check:

- Roof
- Foundation
- HVAC systems
- Plumbing
- Electrical
- Appliances

> **BAKER'S TIP:** Always make your purchase offer contingent on a satisfactory home inspection. Never skip this step because you might regret it in a big (expensive) way.

Insurance: Your New Favorite (Mandatory) Monthly Bill

Your lender will require:

- Homeowners insurance (fire, hazard)
- Flood insurance (if in a flood zone)
- (Possibly) Earthquake insurance in certain areas

Shop early to avoid delays. Some policies require inspections!

Closing Time: What to Expect When You're Finally Adulting

- You'll receive your Closing Disclosure at least three business days before closing.
- Triple-check your loan terms and closing costs before you sign.
- After you sign, funding typically happens the same day or within a few days (varies by state).
- Bring a cashier's check or arrange a wire transfer—personal checks are not accepted.

Congrats—you're now a homeowner!

> **BAKER'S CAVEAT:** Wire transfer fraud has become an increasingly common and costly scam, especially around real estate closings. Here's how it typically works: A day or two before your scheduled closing, you (the buyer) receive an email that looks legitimate, instructing you to wire your deposit or closing funds to a specific account. The message appears to come from your lender or title company, complete with accurate details that make it seem trustworthy.
>
> But it's a scam. Cybercriminals are hacking into title companies' or lenders' systems, stealing sensitive information, and using it to impersonate legitimate parties. If you fall for it, your money could be gone, and often there's no getting it back.
>
> Always verify wire instructions directly with your lender or title company using a trusted phone number and not the one in the suspicious email.

HOAs: The Good, The Bad, and The Surprisingly Petty

If your new home is part of a Homeowners Association (HOA), here's what to expect:

- Monthly or annual dues
- Rules about landscaping, parking, pets, and even holiday decorations
- Possible fines for rule violations

> **BAKER'S TIP:** Always read the HOA rules (called CC&Rs – Covenants, Conditions, and Restrictions) *before* buying. You don't want surprises like "no trucks in the driveway" or "no backyard chickens."
>
> **HOUSING TIP:** Stay informed about your state's property tax laws to ensure you're taking advantage of all available credits and exemptions. For instance, in Arkansas, homeowners can receive a $500 homestead credit. Additionally, those aged 65 and older may qualify to have their property value frozen, potentially saving even more on taxes. Since these laws vary by state, it's important to understand the specific benefits available where you live.

SELLING A HOUSE

Back in 1999, we thought about selling our house and building again (because building a house once just wasn't crazy enough). We listed with a real estate agent but had priced it too high. After six months and zero offers, we pulled it off the market.

In the meantime, we found the perfect plot of land for our next build. On a whim, I stuck a "For Sale By Owner" (FSBO) sign in the yard . . . and waited. Months passed and again, nothing. I eventually tossed the sign in the garage and gave up.

Then one day, I spotted a Cadillac slowly cruising our cul-de-sac. She stopped at the neighbor's house, reading their For Sale sign, and I realized: she has to drive back past our house to leave. I sprinted to the garage, grabbed the FSBO sign, jammed it back into the yard just in time, and sure enough, she slammed on her brakes to read it.

Long story short: Cadillac Lady bought our house—at a premium price!

When my wife and daughter (Lindsey, my future co-author!) got home, I proudly shared my brilliant salesmanship . . . only to be laughed at. Turns out, they had secretly buried a St. Joseph statue in the front yard the day before—a traditional "home-seller's good luck charm." They said it was *his* handiwork, not mine.[9]

Selling a House: Are You Ready?

The selling process starts long before you stick a sign in the yard.

- Walk through your home, inside and out, as if you're seeing it for the first time.
- What needs to be cleaned, painted, repaired, replaced, or tossed?
- First impressions matter. *Curb appeal* matters.

FSBO vs. Hiring a Realtor®: Which Path Should You Take?

You'll need to decide whether to:

- Hire a Realtor® (and pay a typical 6–7% commission)
- Sell it yourself (FSBO) (using for sale by owner websites like ForSaleByOwner.com)

If you're thinking FSBO, ask yourself:

- Do I have the time and energy?
- Am I comfortable negotiating directly with buyers?
- Can I handle legal paperwork like seller disclosures?

> **FSBO WARNING:** Selling your own home sounds great (save money!), but it can be emotionally charged and even unsafe (letting strangers into your home without screening). A great Realtor® can save you time, stress, and legal trouble.

9. The Franciscan Store, *St. Joseph Home Seller Kit*, accessed September 9, 2025, https://thefranciscanstore .org/products/st-joseph-home-seller-kit?srsltid=AfmBOor7cpvW16yeMWFBax8MtPvL02ZcTsoqkM48p0 DUZ-mYLXH7eENR.

Why Realtors® Are Worth It (Most of the Time)

✓ Access to the MLS (Multiple Listing Service) and a network of buyers
✓ Ability to qualify buyers before they waste your time
✓ Negotiation skills that keep things professional, not personal
✓ Handling legal minefields like disclosure forms and contracts
✓ Marketing expertise from killer photos to open houses

Questions to Ask When Hiring a Real Estate Agent

○ Are you a licensed Realtor® (member of the National Association of Realtors®)?
○ What's your track record—how many homes have you sold recently?
○ Who do you represent—the buyer, seller, or both?
○ How long do homes typically sit on the market in this area?
○ How do you plan to market my home (besides putting a sign in the yard)?
○ What is your commission and is it negotiable?

> **BAKER'S TIP:** Don't hire a Realtor® just because they're your friend or cousin. This is a business deal, so treat it like one.

Set the Right Price (Not the Dream Price)

What is your house really worth? It's based on:

- **Recent comparable sales** ("comps") in your area.
- **Current market conditions:** Is it a buyer's market or seller's market?
- **Location, location, location:** Your neighborhood matters.
- **Condition and upgrades:** Good maintenance can mean higher value.

Reality check: Buyers don't care what you "need" from the sale. They care about market value.

> **BAKER'S PRO TIP:** Offering small perks (like covering closing costs or leaving appliances) can sweeten deals without officially dropping your asking price.

Marketing Your Home: Get People in the Door

- ❍ Spruce up landscaping and curb appeal.
- ❍ Take professional-quality photos (or hire someone!).
- ❍ Create a "What I Love About My Home" list for buyers to read because emotions sell!
- ❍ Assist your Realtor® by pointing out hidden perks (great afternoon shade, quiet street, short walk to parks or schools).

Checklist for Sellers: What You'll Need

Before serious buyers come knocking, gather:

- ❍ Warranty deed and title insurance papers
- ❍ Plat map of the property
- ❍ Last 12 months of utility bills
- ❍ Annual property taxes and assessments
- ❍ Termite inspection paperwork (if applicable)
- ❍ List of recent upgrades or repairs
- ❍ Appliance manuals and warranty info
- ❍ Layout showing septic systems, right-of-ways, etc.

Offers, Counteroffers, and Negotiations: Dance Smart

When an offer comes in:

- ❍ Is it close to your asking price?
- ❍ Is it contingent on the buyer selling their own home?
- ❍ Are there multiple offers?

Counteroffers are common. It's not personal, it's just business. (And trust me: using a Realtor® makes negotiating way less awkward.)

Closing the Deal

A signed purchase agreement includes price *plus* terms and conditions, like:

- Buyer's financing approval
- Home inspections
- Appraisals
- Title insurance

Most sales close within 30–45 days after a contract is signed.

> **BAKER'S CHOICE:** If selling FSBO, use a title company to handle your closing. They'll manage paperwork, funds, and title transfers professionally.[10]

What Happens at Closing?

- Buyer's money is wired to the title company.
- Seller is paid (after liens, taxes, fees).
- Title is transferred to the new owner.
- Any pre-paid property taxes are adjusted.
- Buyer officially becomes the new homeowner.

Taxes on Selling Your Home: What You Need to Know

Thanks to the IRS:

- Married couples can exclude up to $500,000 of profit from taxes.
- Single sellers can exclude up to $250,000.
- You must have lived in the home as your primary residence for at least two of the last five years.

> **HEADS-UP:** Tax laws change. Always consult your tax professional before making big assumptions.

---

10. Ben Luthi, "What Does a Title Company Do?" *Experian*, January 4, 2024, https://www.experian.com/blogs
/ask-experian/what-does-title-company-do.

BUILDING A HOUSE— YOU'VE GOT TO BE CRAZY!

We've built three houses during our marriage. Some people joke that you should get marriage counseling *before* building a house, and I wouldn't argue.

Our first and third builds went fine. The second? Let's just call it "The House Build from Hell." Trust me, you'll want to hear that story later.

For this section, we'll assume you're using a bank construction loan, because banks require schedules, inspections, and milestones that protect both the builder and the homeowner.

Steps to Building a House (Without Losing Your Mind)

Step 1: Build for the Next Buyer, Not Just Yourself.
It's easy to design your dream house . . . but remember: life happens.

- ✗ Don't build with only two bedrooms unless you want to limit future buyers.
- ✗ Avoid weird layouts that only make sense to you.
- ✗ Plan for resale, even if you *think* you'll live there forever.

Step 2: Spend Serious Time on the Floor Plan.
Sketch your dream layout first, then take it to a professional.

- **Architect:** Needed if your land has challenges (steep slopes, etc.). More expensive but worth it for complex lots.
- **Draftsman:** Cheaper option if the land is straightforward.

> **IMPORTANT TIP:** Get your ideas sorted before you pay for plans. Every change after the fact = $$$$$. (Trust me.)

Step 3: Hire a General Contractor.

Unless you're a professional builder (or love extreme stress), hire a general contractor.

- ✓ They already have trusted subcontractors lined up.
- ✓ They can spot problems before they snowball.

Finding a Good General Contractor

- Get at least 3–4 bids from contractors recommended by friends.
- Check with suppliers to see if they pay their bills on time.
- Verify that they are licensed and bonded.

5 Red Flags Your Contractor Is in Trouble and Run If You See Them

- ✗ **Too-good-to-be-true pricing.** If their bid is wildly lower than others, there's a reason, and it's probably not a good one.
- ✗ **Constant cash demands without progress.** Asking for large draws while little work is happening = major red flag.
- ✗ **Sketchy payment behavior.** If you hear vendors or subs grumbling about late payments—listen.
- ✗ **Poor communication.** Not returning calls, dodging questions, or giving vague answers is a flashing red light.
- ✗ **Credit card declines or "financial excuses."** If your contractor can't even buy basic materials without a scene at the register—*RUN*.

Quick Guide: What Does "Bonded" Mean?

A bonded contractor has purchased a surety bond, which protects you if they:

- Fail to finish the job
- Skip out on paying subs
- Don't pay for building materials[11]

---

11. Will Kenton, "Understanding Construction Bonds: Types, Requirements, and How They Work," *Investopedia*, last updated August 23, 2025, https://www.investopedia.com/terms/c/construction-bond.asp.

> **BAKER'S WARNING!** Beware of contractors offering "Cost + 10%" deals. Sounds fair, but they have no incentive to control material costs, and you can end up way over budget.[12]

Step 4: Pay Attention to the Money Trail

Always double-check that subs are getting paid. If not, you could get slapped with a mechanic's lien, which is a legal claim against your property.

Stay involved. Ask questions. Don't assume anything.

Step 5: Stay Involved—Every. Single. Day.

You *have* to be on site, watching. It's not fun, it's not glamorous, but it's your investment.

> **True story:** When I was supervising our second house build, a worker once asked what I did for a living. I smiled and said, "Witness Protection Program." (It kept them *very* honest.)

> **BAKER'S CHOICE:** Don't assume the contractor has your best interests at heart. You have to be your own advocate.
>
> **BONUS TIP:** Do Your Homework. There are some great resources like *Chudley and Greeno's Building Construction Handbook* (12th edition).[13] This easy-to-use handbook is a go-to guide for construction students and professionals looking to brush up on their knowledge of all things construction. The 12th edition is updated to include new building methods and regulations while still providing a foundation of basic construction principles, building practices, and regulations. It's cheaper to spend time researching now than to pay for expensive mistakes later.

12. Yash Baheti and Daniel Gray, "*What Is a Cost-Plus Contract in Construction?*," Procore, last updated June 11, 2024, https://www.procore.com/library/cost-plus-contracts#.
13. Roy Chudley, Roger Greeno, and Karl Kovac, *Chudley and Greeno's Building Construction Handbook*, 12th ed. (London: Routledge, 2020).

House Building from Hell

As much as I wish this was fiction . . . it's not.

When we built our second house, we hired a general contractor who gave us a too-good-to-be-true "turnkey" price.

Red flags we missed. He said his price was so low because of "low overhead" and "working on volume." We were paying cash, so we didn't have a bank watching the draw schedule. He kept asking for giant cash draws ($25,000 one week, $30,000 the next), even when little progress was happening.

Still, no red flags seen by the blind, evidently.

Then came divine intervention.

I was at the local lumber store when I spotted our contractor at the register. He tried to pay for supplies with two different declined credit cards—then grudgingly paid cash. I stood there, stunned, like someone had slapped me upside the head.

I immediately told my wife: "No more contractor draws. We'll pay subcontractors directly."

That one decision saved us tens of thousands of dollars.

Turns out, the contractor was deeply behind on payments and headed toward bankruptcy. Because we paid the subs directly, we avoided mechanics' liens against our home.

Moral of the story? When something feels off, act fast. Trust your gut.

PRINCIPLE #11

Protect Your ASSets!

FORE-GOTTEN INSURANCE

Back in the 1980s, I was a broke high school teacher renting a small apartment in South Arkansas. I didn't have much money, but I had great friends and cheap golf.

One afternoon, my buddies Ken and Robby called and said, "Let's hit the links!" We drove across the Arkansas-Louisiana border to a humble 9-hole course in Haynesville; greens fees so cheap they practically paid us to play.

The fourth hole was a par-4 with a sharp 90-degree dogleg right. Ken and Robby played it safe, landing their shots right down the curve. I, on the other hand, sliced mine deep into left field and had to hike (no carts for poor guys like us) to find it.

Feeling bold, or maybe foolish, I grabbed my trusty 3-wood and let it rip. Beautiful contact . . . just one problem—the ball rocketed straight at Ken and Robby.

In panic, I yelled, "DUUUUCK!" (Golf etiquette says yell "FORE!"—but poultry came to mind first.) They squatted immediately, but not quite fast enough, and the ball nailed Ken square in the back.

He laughed it off at first. A few weeks later, X-rays showed a cracked vertebra.

Someone suggested he file a claim against my renter's insurance for medical bills. One tiny hiccup: I didn't have renters insurance. Back then, I figured, "Why bother? I don't own anything valuable."

And that's when I learned the real value of liability coverage. It's not just for replacing your burned-up couch—it's there to protect your assets when your 3-wood turns into a weapon.

Ken fully recovered, and we're still friends.

But he never golfed with me again.

(Honestly . . . smart move.)

> **BAKER'S TIP:** If you rent, get renters insurance. It's cheap and could save you financially (and emotionally) if something weird happens. (It always does.)

WHAT IS INSURANCE?

Insurance is a tool to help protect your financial well-being. It's a contract between you (the insured) and an insurance company, where you pay a regular amount (called a premium) in exchange for financial protection if something unexpected happens, like a fire, car accident, or lawsuit.

When you buy insurance, you're not just following a rule, you're making a strategic decision. You're saying: "If disaster strikes, I won't be alone in paying the bill."

INSURANCE DEALS WITH RISK

Risk is the possibility of loss, harm, or financial setback. While some risk is unavoidable, the smart move is to manage it. You can:

- Avoid it (e.g., never drive)
- Reduce it (e.g., install a smoke detector)
- Accept it (e.g., self-insure)
- Or transfer it—and that's where insurance comes in.

Think of Risk Like a Backpack Full of Bricks

Everyone carries risk on their shoulders. Some carry more than others. Insurance lets you hand some of that heavy load off to a company that can handle it. You still carry the straps, but if the worst happens, you're not crushed under the weight.

WHY THIS MATTERS

Even if you don't want to dig into all the fine print, please take time to read the true stories sprinkled throughout this chapter. They're real, and they show how quickly life can turn upside down, and how powerful the right insurance can be.

Like the dad who saved for 10 years only to lose everything to a house fire . . . but then got a check that let him rebuild. Or the golfer whose routine Sunday round led to a six-figure lawsuit when his stray shot hit someone. These are not scare tactics; they're reminders that good insurance is *peace of mind on paper*.

HOMEOWNERS INSURANCE (AND RENTERS INSURANCE)

A homeowners insurance policy protects your home and the stuff inside it. It also covers your liability if someone is injured on your property, or sometimes even off of it (remember the golf story?).

If you're a renter, you don't own the structure, but you can (and should) get renters insurance, which covers your belongings and personal liability at a low cost.

Baker's Nitty-Gritty of Homeowners Insurance Coverage
Section 1: Property Coverage

Coverage	Description
A	Residence dwelling and attached structures
B	Detached structures (garage, shed) – typically 10% of Coverage A
C	Personal property (furniture, clothes, electronics) – usually 70% of Coverage A if replacement cost
D	Additional living expenses (hotel, food, temporary clothing if you're displaced)

Section 2: Liability Coverage

Coverage	Description
E	Liability insurance for bodily injury or property damage
F	Medical payments for minor injuries to guests (no lawsuit required)

Property Coverage: Replacement Cost vs. Actual Cash Value

When something is damaged or destroyed, your policy may reimburse you in one of two ways:

- **Replacement Cost (RC):** Pays the cost to replace the item *today*— no depreciation.
- **Actual Cash Value (ACV):** Pays the depreciated value of the item at the time of loss.
- **Market Value:** What someone would pay for your house in a competitive market. *Not* relevant for most claims.

> **BAKER'S INSIGHT:** Just because you bought your home for $100,000 doesn't mean you should insure it for $100,000. If it costs $160,000 to rebuild it today, that's what your Coverage A should reflect. Many people are underinsured and don't realize it until it's too late.

> **BAKER'S CHOICE:** Even though the HO-3 policy is the most common homeowners policy, consider upgrading to an HO-5. Why?
>
> - HO-5 covers more: Personal property is covered on an open perils basis (you're covered unless something is specifically excluded).
> - HO-3 covers less: Property is covered on a named perils basis (you're only covered for what's listed).
> - Expanded limits for jewelry, electronics, and high-value items.
> - Losses are reimbursed at replacement cost, not depreciated value.
>
> Check your policy, or ask your agent, if an HO-5 is available. It may cost more, but the added protection can be worth it.

Baker's Homeowners Insurance Checklist

Use this as a quick gut check for your current coverage:

- ○ My dwelling coverage reflects today's *replacement cost*, not what I paid for the house.
- ○ I've reviewed whether I have an HO-3 or HO-5 policy.
- ○ I've documented my belongings (photos/videos of furniture, electronics, etc.).
- ○ I have coverage for high-value items like jewelry, collectibles, or expensive electronics.
- ○ I understand what *isn't* covered (floods, earthquakes, mold).
- ○ I review my policy every 1–2 years to keep up with inflation and life changes.
- ○ I know my deductible and how it affects my premium.

Watch Out for Wind and Hail Deductibles

Many homeowners are surprised to find wind and hail deductibles quietly added to their policy renewals, so it's important to read the fine print.

Unlike your standard homeowners deductible (usually a set dollar amount), a wind/hail deductible kicks in specifically when your home is damaged by windstorms, tornadoes, or hail and it's often calculated as a percentage of your home's insured value.

For example, if your home is insured for $400,000 and you have a 2% wind/hail deductible, you'd be on the hook for the first $8,000 of any wind or hail-related claim before your insurance company pays a dime.

One strong storm could leave you with a hefty bill, so make sure you understand what your policy really covers before bad weather blows through.[1]

KEN WILLIAMS: After the Flames

One evening during dinner with our adult kids, a loud pop sounded and the lights went out. My son-in-law went to check the breaker and came running back shouting, "The house is on fire!" We got everyone (and the pets) out safely, and while 911 was being called, I tried to fight the garage fire with a water hose. Not surprisingly, it didn't help. In hindsight, I should've grabbed our lockbox and car keys, but when your home of 28 years is going up in flames, thinking straight is harder than you'd expect.

The fire spread fast. It was so hot it melted metal. The fire department said if we'd been asleep, our only way out would've been the bedroom window (which was blocked by the bed). We were lucky. No one was hurt. That's what mattered most.

In the following weeks, we scrambled to find temporary housing (thanks to a generous employer) and headed to Walmart at 2 a.m. to buy clothes and toothbrushes. We'd lost everything: home, vehicles, a new travel trailer—all gone.

Then came the real work: insurance. The structure was deemed a total loss and covered up to our policy limit. But the contents? That's a whole different beast. We had to list every single thing we owned, down to socks and spatulas, totaling around 2,000 line items. Each needed details: age, quantity, brand, replacement value, and receipts if they were significant. That list took over five months. Then, after all that, you only get the depreciated value, unless you replace it and prove it with receipts. This process can drag out for up to two years. No receipt, no reimbursement.

---

1. The Horton Group, *Wind/Hail Deductibles and Roof Schedules: What You Need to Know*, March 11, 2025, https://www.thehortongroup.com/resources/wind-hail-deductibles-and-roof-schedules-what-you-need-to-know.

We missed plenty. Pictures or video of our home would've saved months of work and memory strain. Trust me: thinking through every room after it's in ash is no easy task.

People think disasters won't happen to them. I thought that too until I was covered in soot, digging through rubble, wishing I had just one photo album and one more clean shirt.

> **BAKER'S ADVICE:** Once or twice a year, walk through your home and take photos or a video of your personal belongings—not just furniture, but also clothing, electronics, appliances, and anything else of value. This simple habit serves two important purposes: it creates clear proof of ownership for your insurance company in case of a claim, and it helps you remember everything that was lost if you're ever faced with rebuilding after a disaster.

LIABILITY COVERAGE

Your homeowners insurance doesn't just protect your stuff; it protects you from lawsuits. If someone is injured on your property or if you (or a member of your household) accidentally cause damage or harm to someone else, liability coverage kicks in.

Typical Liability Coverage Options

- $100,000
- $300,000
- $500,000

> **BAKER'S CHOICE:** I strongly recommend carrying at least $500,000 in liability coverage and even then, you should consider adding a personal umbrella policy for extra protection (we'll talk more about that later).

What It Covers

Liability coverage helps with:

- Bodily injury to others
- Property damage caused to others
- Legal defense costs, even if you're not at fault

This applies to incidents on and off your property and covers you and other residents in your household.

Real-Life Examples: Why It Matters

- **The Party Host Lawsuit:** You host a party, and one of your guests drinks too much. On their way home, they cause a serious accident. While the injured parties may sue the driver, they can also come after you, claiming you were negligent for serving alcohol and allowing the guest to leave while impaired.
- **Fluffy Gets Feisty:** Your sweet little dog, Fluffy, bites the Amazon delivery driver. Medical bills, missed work, pain and suffering? That's a claim against your liability coverage.
- **Deck Disaster:** You're grilling for friends on your back deck. The deck collapses, injuring two guests. Even if it was an accident, you could still be held responsible and sued.

Liability insurance helps prevent a financial disaster from becoming a life-altering one.

WHAT ABOUT RENTERS INSURANCE?

If you're renting, don't skip this part.

A renters policy is a type of homeowners insurance designed for people who don't own the structure they live in. It still offers Coverage C (Personal Property), Coverage D (Additional Living Expenses), and, importantly, Section 2 Liability Coverage.

Quick Recap: What's NOT Included in a Renters Policy

Coverage	Renters Policy Includes?
Coverage A – Residence Dwelling	✘ Not included
Coverage B – Detached Structures	✘ Not included
Coverage C – Personal Property	✓ Yes
Coverage D – Living Expenses	✓ Yes
Coverage E – Liability	✓ Yes
Coverage F – Medical Payments	✓ Yes

> **BAKER'S CHOICE:** You might be thinking: *"I don't own much—just a mattress, a TV, and a kitchen table. Do I really need renters insurance?"*
>
> Short answer: Yes. Not necessarily because of what you own, but because of what you're liable for. One bad accident, one injury, or one small fire that spreads to your neighbor's unit could cost you thousands or more. Renters insurance is cheap, and the liability protection alone makes it worth every penny.

AUTOMOBILE INSURANCE: NOT JUST FOR WRECKS

An auto insurance policy is a contract between you and an insurance company. You agree to pay a premium, and in return, the insurer agrees to cover certain financial losses if you're involved in an accident or your vehicle is damaged, stolen, or causes harm to others.

Auto insurance isn't just about fender benders; it's about protecting your health, your income, and your assets when something goes wrong on the road.

Core Coverages in an Auto Insurance Policy

Here are the major types of protection included in a standard auto policy:

- **Property Coverage:** Covers damage to or theft of your vehicle.
- **Liability Coverage:** Covers injuries or property damage you cause to others.

- **Medical Coverage:** Pays medical bills for you or your passengers after an accident, including lost wages and funeral costs.

Key Insurance Terms You Should Know

- **Property Damage Liability:** Covers damage you cause to someone else's property—usually their car, but also fences, buildings, signs, etc.
- **Bodily Injury Liability:** Covers costs related to injuries (or death) you cause to others in an accident. This includes:
  - Medical bills
  - Lost wages
  - Pain and suffering
  - Future medical treatment
  - Loss of earning capacity

- **Medical Payments or PIP (Personal Injury Protection):** Pays medical expenses for you and your passengers, regardless of fault. In some cases, it may also cover lost income.
- **Uninsured/Underinsured Motorist (UM/UIM)—Bodily Injury:** Pays for your medical expenses and pain/suffering if the at-fault driver has little or no insurance or flees the scene (hit and run).
- **Uninsured/Underinsured Motorist—Property Damage:** Covers repairs to your vehicle when the other driver doesn't have enough (or any) insurance. Often overlooked, but important.

> **DID YOU KNOW?** As of the last major study by the Insurance Information Institute, about 1 in 8 drivers in the US had no auto insurance. That number doesn't include those who are *underinsured*, which is even more common due to low state minimum coverage limits.[2]

---

2. Insurance Research Council, *One in Eight Drivers Uninsured*, news release, March 22, 2021, https://www.insurance-research.org/sites/default/files/downloads/UM%20NR%20032221.pdf.

Baker's Nitty-Gritty of Auto Insurance
Property Coverage

Type	What It Covers
Collision	Repairs or replacement if your car hits another car or object
Comprehensive	Damage from non-collision events like fire, hail, vandalism, theft, or even a falling tree limb (or asteroid, seriously)
Towing	Optional, usually reimburses $50–$100; skip if you already have roadside assistance like AAA
Rental Reimbursement	Optional; pays for a rental car while your vehicle is being repaired after an accident

> **BAKER'S CHOICE!** Consider raising your collision/comprehensive deductibles to $1,000+ to lower premiums, especially if you wouldn't file a claim for a small repair anyway.
>
> If your car is 10+ years old, and its actual cash value is low, it might not be worth paying for physical damage coverage.
>
> Never drop liability coverage. It's required and financially critical.

Liability Coverage

Having enough liability coverage is one of the smartest financial decisions you can make. Most states require only minimal amounts, like $25,000/$50,000/$25,000 (split limits), which won't go far in a serious accident.

Split Limits Example	What It Covers
$25,000	Max paid per person injured
$50,000	Max paid for all people injured
$25,000	Max for property damage caused

Combined Single Limit policies offer one larger pool of money to cover both bodily injury and property damage—much more flexible and often more protective.

Case Study: The Flippin' Mess

Carella lives in Flippin, Arkansas (yes, it's real). One distracted afternoon, she runs a stop sign while texting and playing with her dogs. She causes a multi-car pileup, injures two pedestrians, destroys a fence, and slams into someone's house.

Injuries
- 4 car occupants: $80,000
- 2 pedestrians: $7,000
- Total Bodily Injury: $87,000

Property Damage
- 2 cars: $50,000
- Fence: $1,000
- House: $50,000
- Total Property Damage: $101,000

Grand Total: *$188,000 in damages*

But Carella only had Arkansas's minimum split-limit policy:

- $25,000 per person
- $50,000 total bodily injury
- $25,000 total property damage
- Max payout by insurance: $75,000

That leaves $113,000 uncovered, and the injured parties will come after her.

What Happens When You're Underinsured?

When insurance isn't enough, the rest of the financial responsibility falls on you. Attorneys may perform an asset check to see what they can legally collect real estate, bank accounts, and even future wages.

In short: you're exposed.

> **BAKER'S CHOICE!** I recommend a minimum of $500,000 in com-
> bined single limit liability coverage, plus $500,000 in uninsured/
> underinsured motorist protection (including property damage).
> High coverage gives your insurer more room to settle claims with-
> out dragging you into court.
>
> And yes, add a personal umbrella policy for an extra layer of
> protection. You'll sleep better knowing you're covered, even on your
> worst day.

PERSONAL UMBRELLA POLICY: YOUR FINANCIAL SAFETY NET

A personal umbrella policy is an extra layer of liability protection that sits on top of your existing insurance—homeowners, auto, boat, rental property, and more. It kicks in when the limits on those policies are maxed out.

Umbrella policies typically come in $1 million increments, and they're designed to protect your current assets and your future income from large claims or lawsuits.

Who Needs an Umbrella Policy?

While anyone can benefit from this protection, umbrella insurance is especially important if you:

- Own property (especially multiple properties)
- Have a high income or growing net worth
- Have kids or teens (drivers, social media users, etc.)
- Engage in higher-risk activities or hobbies
- Host guests or parties at your home
- Own anything that could cause injury to others (see below)

Baker's Nitty-Gritty of Umbrella Coverage

As your assets grow, your risk grows too. You may not think you're a lawsuit target, but if you cause a serious car accident or someone gets badly injured on your property, you absolutely could be.

An umbrella policy can:

- Cover damages beyond your underlying policy limits
- Pay for legal defense costs
- Help settle claims before they escalate
- Provide protection against personal liability lawsuits that most people never think about

Peace of mind is cheap. Umbrella policies are surprisingly affordable—typically around $200–$400 per year for the first $1 million in coverage. Rates go up slightly for additional millions, but the protection is exponential.

Real-Life Scenarios Where an Umbrella Policy Matters

- **You have a pool:** Someone slips and breaks their neck. Medical bills and a lawsuit exceed your homeowners liability limits.
- **You cause a major car accident:** Multiple people are injured. Your auto policy maxes out, but the costs keep coming. The umbrella policy covers the excess.
- **You own a boat or jet ski:** You hit a swimmer or another vessel. The damages exceed your watercraft liability policy.
- **You have teenage drivers:** Young drivers = higher risk. One wrong move and you're financially exposed.
- **You coach a youth sports team:** You're falsely accused of inappropriate behavior. Even if you're innocent, the legal fees can be crushing.
- **You serve on a nonprofit board:** You're sued for mismanagement or misuse of funds. Your personal assets may be at risk if the organization's insurance doesn't cover it all.

> **BAKER'S CHOICE!** If you have "toys"—like a trampoline, ATV, side-by-side, boat, or swimming pool—you need a personal umbrella policy. If you drive a lot, host guests frequently, volunteer, or simply want to protect your financial future, umbrella coverage is a smart move. If your net worth is climbing, this is a no-brainer. Don't build wealth without protecting it.

I was hired by Oak Hills Church (San Antonio, Texas) in September 1988 as the Youth Minister. Six years later, I transitioned to Minister of Involvement, eventually becoming Executive Minister. During that time, the church grew rapidly, from 550 to over 5,000 in weekly attendance, and our staff expanded from 10 to more than 20. I was responsible for the budget and all hiring, and I realized that as we grew, we needed to offer better staff benefits, including disability insurance. After researching and implementing a policy, I remember thinking it might be one of the best decisions of my tenure.

Ironically, just a few years later in 2002, I became the first to use the disability benefit after suffering a hemorrhagic stroke. The pain and long-term effects made it impossible to continue in my demanding role, so I stepped down and cycled through three less intensive ministry positions, eventually working with Singles Ministry. Finally, I accepted the reality that I needed to go on disability—the very program I helped create.

I turned 65 five years ago, and the disability coverage ended then. But for over a decade, that policy supported my family and gave me the time to heal. In 2015, I fulfilled a lifelong dream: teaching two Freshman Bible classes as an adjunct professor at Abilene Christian University. That opportunity, and the stability behind it, wouldn't have been possible without the foresight of establishing a safety net for others . . . and myself.

DISABILITY INSURANCE: PROTECTING YOUR MOST VALUABLE ASSET—YOUR INCOME

Imagine losing your paycheck overnight—not because you lost your job, but because you were injured or got sick and couldn't work for weeks, months, or even years. How would you pay your bills, support your family, or stay financially afloat?

That's where disability insurance comes in.

What Is Disability Insurance?

Disability insurance provides replacement income if you become unable to work due to injury or illness. It typically pays a percentage of your gross income, most often up to 66%, to help cover your living expenses while you're out of work.

> **IMPORTANT DISTINCTION:** Disability insurance is not the same as workers' compensation. Workers' comp only covers injuries or illnesses that happen on the job. Most disabling events, however, occur outside of work, like a car accident, back injury, stroke, or cancer diagnosis.

Baker's Nitty-Gritty of Disability Insurance Coverage

Do I Really Need Disability Insurance?

Unless you're independently wealthy or have a trust fund set up by Uncle Jed Clampett, the answer is: yes, you do.

Here's why: Over 61 million US adults (or 1 in 4) report having a disability according to 2022 Centers for Disease Control (CDC) data.[3]

Where Can You Get Coverage?

You typically have two options:

1. **Through Your Employer** as an Employee Benefit (e.g., group disability insurance policy)
   - Usually more affordable
   - Often guaranteed issue (no medical exam)
   - Downsides? Not portable. You lose the coverage if you leave your job.

2. **Individual Policy**
   - Follows you wherever you work
   - Offers customizable features (more on that below)
   - Typically requires medical underwriting
   - More expensive, but much more flexible

---

3. Centers for Disease Control and Prevention, *Prevalence of Disabilities and Health Care Access by Disability Status and Type Among Adults*, last updated April 11, 2025, https://www.cdc.gov/disability-and-health/articles-documents/disabilities-health-care-access.html.

> **BAKER'S CHOICE:** If you can afford it, having your own individual policy is a smart long-term move. You'll never have to worry about gaps in coverage when changing jobs.

Are Disability Benefits Taxable?

- If your employer pays the premium, any disability payments you receive are taxable.
- If you pay the premium with after-tax dollars, the benefits are tax-free.

> **WHY IT MATTERS:** If your monthly disability benefit is only 66% of your income and it's taxed, your real take-home could drop below 50%, potentially creating financial hardship right when you're least able to handle it.

Five Key Questions to Ask Before Buying Individual Disability Insurance

Question	What to Know
1. How much is the benefit?	Typically up to 66% of your gross monthly income
2. What's the elimination period?	How long you wait before benefits kick in (30, 60, or 90 days)
3. How long does coverage last?	Options include 2 years, 5 years, or until age 67
4. Is it "own occupation" coverage?	This matters! "Own occ" protects you if you can't work in *your specific job*
5. How much will it cost?	Premiums typically run 1–3% of your income, depending on coverage and riders

Social Security and Disability

Technically, the Social Security Administration offers disability benefits. In practice? They're very hard to qualify for and often take months or years to get approved.

> **BAKER'S CHOICE:** Create your own My Social Security Account today.[4] It lets you:
>
> - Review your earnings history
> - Estimate future disability or retirement benefits
> - Protect your identity from fraudulent claims
>
> Years ago, just out of college, I checked my SSA earnings and saw two years with zero reported income, despite receiving W-2s. Turns out the company's bookkeeper wasn't forwarding payroll taxes. I submitted my W-2s, and the SSA fixed my records. Not sure what happened to the bookkeeper, but I hope the IRS had a chat!

Where to Start Shopping for Disability Insurance?

Disability insurance can be complex. It's essential to work with a trusted, independent insurance professional, who can walk you through:

- "Own occupation" definitions
- Elimination periods
- Optional riders (like cost-of-living adjustments or residual income)
- Tax considerations

> **BAKER'S CHOICE:** Don't wing this. Your income is likely your greatest asset and without it, everything else is at risk. Work with a specialist to build a policy that fits your life, your career, and your budget.

---

4. Social Security Administration, *my Social Security*, https://www.ssa.gov/myaccount/.

LIFE INSURANCE:
PLANNING FOR THE PEOPLE YOU LOVE

A life insurance policy is a contract between you and an insurance company. In exchange for premium payments, the insurer promises to pay a death benefit to your named beneficiaries when you die. That lump-sum payment can be used for anything, such as mortgage payments, childcare, funeral costs, or simply to help your loved ones stay financially stable after you're gone.

Life insurance gives your family breathing room when they need it most.

MIKE RYBURN: Legacy After Loss

The first thing I remember clearly was waking up to a house full of women from our church. It was 1959. I was five years old and had no idea what was going on. My brother was seven, my sister just three. Our mother was being comforted, given sedatives and tranquilizers. Confused and scared, we stayed close together, trying to make sense of the silence and whispers.

Eventually, I overheard the words that changed everything: our father, just 33 years old, had been killed in a car accident.

What none of us knew at the time was that my father had recently purchased a new life insurance policy for $125,000 to replace an older one, also worth $125,000, that hadn't yet expired. Because both policies were still active at the time of his death, my mother received a total payout of $250,000. In today's dollars, that's the equivalent of about $2.7 million.

Grieving and overwhelmed, my mom went to a lawyer for guidance. He advised her to invest conservatively, placing a portion of the money into certificates of deposit and the rest into a trust to fund our future education.

Because we were so young, the trust had time to grow. It eventually paid for all our college and graduate school expenses. My mother lived off the interest for the rest of her life and never had to work while raising us. When she passed, she still had the original principal, which she left to us.

Our father's foresight didn't just protect us; it gave us the stability, education, and future we never could've had otherwise. That single decision, made quietly and responsibly, changed the course of our lives.

Why People Buy Life Insurance

Life insurance is for those left behind—spouses, children, aging parents, or anyone who depends on your income or caregiving.

Common reasons people purchase life insurance:

- To pay off a mortgage or other debts
- To cover funeral and burial costs
- To replace lost income
- To provide for children's education
- To support a disabled or elderly dependent
- To replace the economic value of a stay-at-home spouse
- To leave a charitable gift
- To create an estate plan

Most Overlooked Need: A stay-at-home spouse or partner may not earn income, but their contribution (childcare, transportation, cleaning, etc.) has real financial value. If that person were gone, you'd likely need to hire help, and life insurance can make that possible.

Do I Need Life Insurance?

If your death would cause financial stress for someone including your spouse, kids, business partner, or aging parent, then yes, you probably need life insurance.

How Much Life Insurance Do I Need?

Some advisors suggest 7–10 times your annual income as a general rule of thumb. For example:

$100,000 income = $700,000 to $1 million in life insurance

But that's just a starting point. A better approach is to ask: *What would I want this policy to accomplish?*
Consider:

- How long your dependents will need income
- Whether you want to pay off your mortgage or fund college
- Whether your spouse works or stays home
- If you'll leave behind significant debts

Baker's Choice! Go with Term Life Insurance

Term *life insurance* is straightforward:

- You choose a term (e.g. 10, 20, 30 years).
- You pay a fixed premium.
- If you die during that term, the policy pays out.
- No cash value, no gimmicks, just pure protection.

It's also much cheaper than "cash value" or "permanent" policies like whole life or universal life.

Why I Don't Recommend Cash Value Life Insurance (and You Should Be Skeptical Too)

Insurance agents may pitch whole life, universal life, or variable life as an "investment." Here's why you should think twice:

- ✗ **Higher premiums:** often 10–15x more than term
- ✗ **Complex illustrations:** hard to understand, often overly optimistic
- ✗ **Only the face value is paid at death:** not the cash value *and* the death benefit
- ✗ **Big commissions for agents:** up to 70–90% of your first year's premium
- ✗ **Hefty surrender charges if you cancel early**
- ✗ **High fees:** mortality and investment fees can erode returns

A student once told me an insurance agent advised putting money into a universal life policy instead of their 401(k). That's a red flag. Life insurance is not a substitute for a retirement plan.

Where (and How) to Buy Term Life Insurance

Look for:

- Competitive premiums
- Reputable, highly rated company (A or better from A.M. Best)
- A policy that fits your needs (term length, coverage amount, convertibility)

> **BAKER'S CAVEAT:** Be cautious when shopping online. Many quote engines show "super preferred" or "preferred" rates, but only a small percentage of applicants actually qualify for those. After your medical exam and underwriting, your final premium could be much higher.
>
> In my experience, few people qualify for the top-tier rate class. Be prepared for an honest health screening and medical history check.

Baker's Choice! Policies to Think Twice About

- **Credit Life Insurance:** Covers debts like a car loan or credit card if you die. It's wildly overpriced—up to 50x more than regular term life.
- **Cancer / Dread Disease / Indemnity Plans:** Pay out a set amount for a specific diagnosis or treatment. These often duplicate what your health insurance already covers.
- **Child Life Insurance:** This one's tough. Most children don't generate income, so life insurance isn't necessary beyond burial expenses. Instead, insure the breadwinners.
- **Mortgage Life Insurance:** Also called decreasing term. It pays off your mortgage if you die—but the coverage shrinks over time, while the premium often stays the same. Expensive and less flexible than regular term insurance.

HEALTH INSURANCE: YOUR SHIELD AGAINST MEDICAL BANKRUPTCY

In the US, healthcare costs are one of the leading causes of personal bankruptcy,[5] and yet, some people still wonder whether they really need health insurance. Let's make this clear: *Yes, you need it.*

Unless you're extremely wealthy and can self-insure against the risk of a $200,000 hospital stay or a six-figure surgery, health insurance is essential.

Where Do Most People Get Health Insurance?

Most people are covered under a group health insurance plan offered by their employer. These plans are generally the best deal in terms of cost and coverage because:

✓ Your employer often pays a portion of your premium.
✓ There's strength in numbers (group bargaining power).
✓ Medical underwriting is often not required.

If that's not available, for instance if you're self-employed, work part-time, or your employer doesn't offer a plan, you'll need to get individual health insurance, usually through the HealthCare.gov marketplace or a private insurer.

---

5. Jay Eisenstock, "The financial toll of medical bills: Why healthcare costs lead to bankruptcy | Viewpoint," *Chief Healthcare Executive,* April 27, 2025, https://www.chiefhealthcareexecutive.com/view/the-financial -toll-of-medical-bills-why-healthcare-costs-lead-to-bankruptcy-viewpoint.

Types of Health Insurance Plans

Each plan has trade-offs in terms of cost, access, and flexibility. Here's a breakdown of the most common options:

Indemnity or Fee-for-Service (also called POS)

- Most flexible: See any doctor or specialist you want
- No referrals needed
- Insurance pays a portion, you pay the rest
- Usually the most expensive and harder to find today

Health Maintenance Organization (HMO)

- Lower cost, but more restrictions
- You must choose a primary care physician (PCP) who manages your care
- Referrals are required to see specialists
- Care is only covered in-network (except emergencies)

PCPs are called "gatekeepers" for a reason—no referral, no coverage.

Preferred Provider Organization (PPO)

- More flexible than an HMO
- You can go out of network, but you'll pay more
- No need for a referral to see specialists
- Often preferred for people who travel or want provider choice

Health Savings Account (HSA) + High-Deductible Health Plan (HDHP)

- Requires enrollment in a high-deductible plan
- You contribute pre-tax money to an HSA to pay for medical costs
- Funds grow tax-free
- Withdrawals for qualified medical expenses are tax-free
- Often paired with employer contributions
- Funds roll over year to year and can be invested

- Triple tax benefit: Pre-tax contributions + tax-free growth + tax-free withdrawals
- Great option for young, healthy, or high-income earners looking for both coverage and a tax-advantaged savings tool[6]

> **BAKER'S CHOICE:** If you're young and healthy, an HSA + HDHP combo is hard to beat. It's a powerful way to lower premiums while building long-term savings for future medical expenses or even early retirement healthcare needs.

TERRY POTTER: The Best $150 I Ever Spent

Years ago, our son Matthew dropped out of college, making him ineligible for our health insurance. This was before the age-26 rule, so we urged him to get coverage on his own. Like many young adults, he didn't see the point because he never got sick, so why pay for insurance?

We stayed on him, but he kept putting it off. Finally, as the semester wrapped up and he still hadn't followed through, I bought a short-term policy myself: $150 for a high-deductible, catastrophic coverage plan.

Three weeks later, on December 28, 2011, Matthew rolled his car leaving Stillwater, Oklahoma, on his way home for Christmas. He suffered a broken neck and a serious head injury. First responders life-flighted him to Oklahoma City, where a neurosurgeon (miraculously in town for just that day) performed emergency brain surgery.

He survived, recovered fully, and today he's perfectly healthy. But his medical bills totaled more than $350,000.

Thanks to that $150 policy, it was all covered.

Without it, we would've drained our life savings. I would have gladly paid anything for my son's recovery, but that tiny investment saved us from financial devastation.

---

6. Rob Williams, "Potential Long-Term Benefits of Investing Your HSA," *Charles Schwab*, March 12, 2025, https://www.schwab.com/learn/story/potential-long-term-benefits-investing-your-hsa.

Buying Health Insurance on Your Own

If you can't get coverage through work, go online to use the Affordable Care Act Marketplace at HealthCare.gov. It lets you:

- Compare policies
- Apply for premium subsidies (based on income)
- Purchase directly from insurers or through a broker

Thanks to the ACA, insurers can no longer deny you coverage for pre-existing conditions.

What Happens When You Leave a Job? (Hello, COBRA)

If you lose or leave your job, you may be eligible to continue your current group plan for a limited time under COBRA (Consolidated Omnibus Budget Reconciliation Act).[7]

COBRA Coverage

- Keeps your same plan
- Lasts typically up to 18 months
- You pay the full premium (employer portion + your portion + admin fee)
- Good choice if you're between jobs or want to keep your doctors

When to Use COBRA

- ✓ You or your dependents would otherwise go without coverage.
- ✓ You love your current plan and providers.
- ✓ You're in a gap period before starting a new job.

When to Skip COBRA

- ✗ You can get coverage through a spouse or parent.
- ✗ You qualify for a better or cheaper plan on the marketplace.

See more FAQs at DOL COBRA FAQs.[8]

---

7. U.S. Department of Labor, *Continuation of Health Coverage (COBRA)*, accessed September 9, 2025, https://www.dol.gov/general/topic/health-plans/cobra.

8. Ibid.

Health-Share Plans: Faith-Based, But Risky

Health-share plans, often promoted by religious groups, are not insurance. Members agree to pool money and cover each other's medical expenses, but:

- ✘ They may not cover pre-existing conditions.
- ✘ There's no legal guarantee they'll pay anything.
- ✘ They're not regulated like traditional health insurance.

Proceed with caution. If the monthly cost sounds too good to be true, read the fine print carefully. These plans have left some members holding the bag for massive bills.

BAKER'S CHOICE:

- Stick with ACA-compliant coverage if possible
- Use HSA + HDHP if you're healthy and want a tax-advantaged option
- Think twice before trusting a health-share plan as your only safety net
- If you're in between jobs, evaluate COBRA vs Marketplace options carefully

---

Individual Professional Liability Insurance: Protection for Your Career

If you offer advice, provide a service, or interact with clients or the public in a professional capacity, you may be one mistake, or one accusation, away from a lawsuit.

That's where individual professional liability insurance comes in.

Also known as errors and omissions (E&O) coverage, this type of policy protects you personally in case someone claims your professional advice or actions caused them harm physically, financially, or otherwise.

What Does It Cover?

Professional liability insurance covers:

- Negligence or mistakes in your professional work

- Failure to perform a service
- Errors or omissions in advice or recommendations
- Bodily injury, property damage, or financial losses caused by your actions—or inaction

In short: if someone believes you did your job poorly, missed something, or harmed them through your professional service, this coverage is your financial safety net.

> **IMPORTANT:** This coverage protects *you*, not your employer or business.

Who Needs It?

You might be surprised how many people benefit from this type of policy. It's not just doctors and lawyers.

Common Professions That Should Consider E&O Coverage

- Pharmacists
- Nurses and nurse practitioners
- Physicians and surgeons
- Dentists and hygienists
- Physical and occupational therapists
- Chiropractors
- Accountants and tax preparers
- Teachers and professors
- Real estate agents and appraisers
- Engineers and architects
- Insurance agents and financial advisors
- Home inspectors and land surveyors

If your job involves advising, diagnosing, documenting, or managing risk—this applies to you.

- **Pharmacist:** Fills the wrong dosage on a prescription or accidentally discloses a patient's protected health information.
- **Teacher:** Fails to supervise a student on the playground, resulting in injury or faces allegations of inappropriate behavior, even if false.
- **Accountant:** Files a return incorrectly, leading the client to pay unexpected taxes, penalties, or interest.
- **Home Inspector:** Misses a structural flaw or roof defect, resulting in major post-sale repairs for the buyer.
- **Land Surveyor:** Errors on a property line result in a home being built partially on someone else's lot.

What About My Employer's Insurance?

Many people assume their employer's coverage will protect them. But here's the reality:

- Your employer's business policy may not include you personally.
- Coverage can be limited, expire, or become invalid if the claim involves something:
  - Outside your scope of work.
  - That occurred after you left the job.
  - That your employer failed to properly insure.

And your homeowners insurance? It almost always excludes anything job-related, including freelance or side work.

Bottom line: If you're licensed, credentialed, or compensated for your expertise, you need your own liability protection.

How to Get Covered

Start by checking with your professional association. Many have partnerships with insurers offering:

- Discounted rates
- Tailored coverage for your profession
- Pre-vetted insurance providers

You can also go through:

- An independent insurance agent who represents multiple carriers
- Direct providers like Progressive, biBerk (a Berkshire Hathaway Company), Chubb, Hiscox, State Farm, or other established companies

Ask about:

- Occurrence vs. claims-made policies—Occurrence is broader coverage. If available, choose it over claims-made.[9]
- Coverage limits (e.g., $1 million per claim / $3 million aggregate per policy period)
- Whether coverage applies after hours, off-site, or during volunteer work

> **BAKER'S CHOICE:** If your profession puts you at risk for lawsuits, whether due to patient interactions, financial advice, or classroom supervision, don't rely on someone else's insurance policy to protect you.
>
> Get your own individual professional liability policy. Make sure it follows you, not your employer. Sleep better knowing you're covered at work, after hours, and everywhere in between.

PROTECT YOUR ASSETS IN A DIVORCE

I'm not an attorney. I haven't been divorced. But after decades in the financial world and plenty of time observing friends, relatives, and clients, I've seen how emotionally, physically, and financially brutal a divorce can be.

This book is about building and protecting wealth. So, as uncomfortable as it may be to talk about, we can't ignore one of the biggest threats to your financial foundation: divorce.

---

9. Daniel Liberto, "*Occurrence Policy: What It Is, How It Works, Pros and Cons,*" *Investopedia*, last updated August 6, 2023, https://www.investopedia.com/terms/o/occurrence-policy.asp.

The Reality of Divorce in America

According to the American Psychological Association:[10]

- More than 90% of people in Western cultures marry by age 50.
- 40–50% of marriages end in divorce.[11]
- The divorce rate is even higher for second and third marriages.[12]

And while healthy marriages can be great for your finances and emotional well-being, divorce can wreck both, especially if you're not prepared.

Baker's Nitty-Gritty: How to Protect Your Assets in a Divorce

Whether you're happily married, newly engaged, or considering a separation, these tips apply to everyone:

1. Get a Lawyer (Even in an "Amicable" Divorce)

What starts out friendly often turns contentious once money and emotions collide. You need someone who's looking out just for you. Don't assume fairness will just happen.

2. Get Organized—Fast

Make copies of everything:

- Wills and trusts
- Tax returns
- Bank and brokerage accounts
- Credit card statements
- Mortgage and loan documents
- Property and vehicle titles

Being organized now saves you later, financially and legally.

---

10. Anna Miller, "Can this marriage be saved?" *Monitor on Psychology* 44, no. 4 (April 2013): 42, https://www.apa .org/monitor/2013/04/marriage.

11. Petrelli Previtera, LLC, *Divorce 2022 Statistics*, January 9, 2023, https://www.petrellilaw.com/divorce-statistics -for-2022/.

12. Ibid.

3. Open a Bank Account in Your Own Name

You'll need money for:

- Legal fees
- Court filings
- Personal expenses

Tell your attorney you're doing this. Don't try to hide money. If you're caught, it could ruin your case and your credibility.

4. Do an Asset Search (Yes, Even on Your Spouse)

Financial infidelity is real. One friend discovered, mid-divorce, that her husband had secret bank accounts in his name only, despite earning five times her income and controlling all the household bills.

The Gender Gap in Financial Awareness

According to a UBS study:[13]

- 56% of married women leave investment decisions to their husbands.
- Among millennial women, that number jumps to 61%.
- 80% of women will end up alone.
- 98% of divorcees and widows would advise other women to take an active role in finance now.

That's a problem because women are:

- Living longer
- Controlling more wealth
- Still often left vulnerable during divorce or widowhood

> **BAKER'S CHOICE:** Whether you're married, single, or somewhere in between, you need to know where your money is, you need to know how it works, and you need to have access to it.

---

13. UBS Global Wealth Management, *UBS Reveals Top Reason Millennials Are Saving More Than Any Previous Generation*, news release, May 14, 2018, https://www.ubs.com/global/de/media/display-page-ndp/en -20180514-ubs-reveals-top-reason.html.

Divorce is a storm. But you don't have to lose your financial house when it hits.

PROTECT YOUR ASSETS FROM IDENTITY THEFT

Some personal safety habits become second nature, like buckling your seatbelt or watching your back in a dark parking lot. But when it comes to digital and financial safety, we often let our guard down until it's too late.

Let me share a quick story.

My daughter did everything right while traveling through Guatemala. She researched the safest ATMs, asked around, and took precautions. But despite her vigilance, her debit card was cloned at an ATM, and hundreds of dollars were stolen and withdrawn in $300 chunks.

The only reason she caught it in time? She regularly checked her account balance. Prevention matters, but early detection is everything.

The Scope of the Problem

According to the Federal Trade Commission (FTC), identity theft and fraud are massive, growing problems:[14]

- In 2018, the FTC processed 1.4 million fraud reports, totaling $1.48 billion in losses.
- The top categories: imposter scams, debt collection fraud, and identity theft.
- Credit card fraud was the most reported form of identity theft with over 167,000 cases of accounts opened with stolen info.

---

14. Federal Trade Commission, *Imposter Scams Top Complaints Made to FTC in 2018*, news release, February 28, 2019, https://www.ftc.gov/news-events/news/press-releases/2019/02/imposter-scams-top-complaints-made-ftc-2018.

MARY CONLAN: A Costly Lesson

When my kids were younger, they were always asking for cash to go out with friends. I worried they'd lose it or need more while they were out and I wouldn't be able to help. To make things easier (and to teach them responsibility), I opened separate debit card accounts for each of them. These accounts were in their names but were ultimately still tied to mine. I started this when they were in middle school and left the setup in place through high school and beyond. It seemed to be working.

Until it wasn't.

One of my daughters was about 18 when she fell for a scam. A stranger convinced her to deposit a $30,000 check, promising she could keep $5,000 if she gave them the rest. She was still naive and, despite her age, didn't fully grasp how banking worked. Three days later, I started getting text alerts; her account was overdrawn. When I called to ask what was going on, she was evasive at first, scared and ashamed. Eventually, she told me everything.

I took her straight to the police station. She cried the entire way, realizing she'd been scammed and could actually face jail time. The officer explained the check was fake and the only way to avoid criminal charges was to pay the full amount back. She's been paying it off for years now and still owes $17,000, but she hasn't missed a single payment.

Even though the account was technically hers, the impact hit all of us. The bank emptied my checking and savings accounts, plus the balances from my other kids' accounts, to cover the overdraft. Once we set up a formal payment plan, the withdrawals stopped and the account was secured, but the damage was done.

Looking back, I wish I had just handed them a $20 bill and hoped for the best. It might've been lost, but it wouldn't have cost us $30,000. Kids make mistakes, but some come with very real, very adult consequences.

Baker's Choice: Use a Commercial Service (But Choose Wisely)

I use Zander Insurance for identity theft protection, not because they monitor my credit (many services do that) but because they include restoration services. That means if something goes wrong, I don't have to do the legwork myself.

From their site:

"Zander ID Theft Solutions takes over all the recovery work, providing white-glove service through a Certified Recovery Specialist."

That peace of mind is worth the premium to me.

Don't Want to Pay for a Service?
Here's What You Can (and Should) Do

If you'd rather skip the monthly fee, there are plenty of powerful steps you can take on your own to protect your identity. Here's how:

1. Monitor Your Credit (for Free)

You're entitled to one free credit report per year from each of the three credit bureaus. Go to AnnualCreditReport.com—the only *official* site.

> **BAKER'S PRO TIP:** Instead of pulling all three reports at once, stagger them every 4 months to monitor year-round.

You can also use tools like Credit Karma to:

- Check your scores for free
- Get alerts when something changes on your reports
- Learn how to improve your credit

2. Review Your Account Statements Regularly

Log into your:

- Credit cards
- Bank accounts
- Investment and retirement accounts
- Health insurance EOBs (Explanation of Benefits)

Review transactions regularly. Often, fraudulent activity shows up here before it hits your credit report.

3. Shred Old Documents

Don't just toss bank statements or tax documents in the trash. Shred them. Check out the FTC's guide: What to Shred and When.[15]

4. Freeze Your Credit

This is one of the most effective, underused identity theft defenses. A credit freeze blocks new accounts from being opened in your name—period.

Freezes are free and can be lifted temporarily if you need a loan or open a new account.

Contact all three bureaus separately to freeze your credit:

- Equifax: 800-685-1111
- Experian: 888-397-3742
- TransUnion: 888-909-8872

Learn more: FTC Credit Freeze FAQs[16]

BAKER'S CHOICE: I do all of these:

- I use Zander for white-glove restoration services.
- I've frozen my credit at all three bureaus.
- I monitor accounts regularly and shred everything sensitive.

Final Word: Trust . . . But Check

You don't need to live in fear, but you do need to pay attention. Identity theft won't go away, and no system is foolproof, but layered defenses, good habits, and a little vigilance go a long way.

---

15. Federal Trade Commission, *Shredding Infographic*, April 2015, https://consumer.ftc.gov/articles/0527 -shredding-infographic.

16. Federal Trade Commission, *Credit Freeze FAQs*, September 2017, https://dalecu.com/wp-content/uploads /2022/03/FTC-Credit-Freeze-FAQs.pdf.

FROM PURPLE RAIN TO PROBATE PAIN

When the legendary musician Prince passed away in 2016, he left no will. What followed was a $150+ million mess that took over six years to untangle. Lawyers made a fortune, the IRS grabbed a big slice, and his family spent years in court instead of grieving in peace, all because he didn't have a plan.[17]

Now, you don't have to wear purple velvet or own a vault of unreleased hits to create estate drama. Even if your "estate" is just a pickup truck, a fishing boat, and a slightly used recliner, things can get sideways fast without the right paperwork.

To help keep your family out of probate court (and off Judge Judy), here's a solid estate planning checklist from my friend and attorney, Ledly Jennings, the same guy who set up my own plan. Trust me, it's way easier to do this now than to leave your loved ones guessing later.

LEDLY JENNINGS, J.D.: Why the Right Documents Matter More Than a Will

Let's start with a hard truth: life doesn't always give warnings. A diagnosis, a car accident, a sudden death—these things often arrive without notice. When they do, your family will either have a plan . . . or a mess. Estate planning is about more than protecting your money. It's about protecting your people, your values, and your legacy.

Too often, people focus on a Last Will and Testament, assuming that's the key document everyone needs. And while a will is important, it only comes into play after death. The truth is, some of the most critical decisions your loved ones may need to make will happen while you're still alive but unable to speak for yourself. That's where the right documents, beyond just the will, can make all the difference.

Take the Durable Power of Attorney. This one document can allow someone you trust to handle your finances if you become incapacitated. Without it, banks, insurance companies, even Social Security may refuse to talk to your spouse or children. I had a client whose son found himself in exactly that

---

17. Legacy Plan, "Prince's music and lack of an estate plan are conflicting legacies," October 25, 2024, accessed September 9, 2025, https://legacyassuranceplan.com/articles/intestacy/prince-estate-intestacy-laws.

position. His mother had a stroke, and no one would speak to him. He couldn't access her accounts, pay her bills, or even get information about her care because she hadn't signed a Durable Power of Attorney.

Healthcare documents are just as important. If you can't speak for yourself, a Healthcare Power of Attorney gives someone you trust the ability to make medical decisions on your behalf. A HIPAA Authorization allows access to your medical records. A Living Will outlines your wishes for end-of-life care so your family isn't left guessing during an already painful time.

Now, back to that will. One of the biggest misconceptions about wills is that they avoid probate. They don't. In fact, a will guarantees probate—a slow, costly, and public court process to distribute your assets. Anything held in your name alone will go through probate, even with a perfectly drafted will.

There are better options. Beneficiary designations are one simple way to bypass probate. By naming beneficiaries on things like life insurance, retirement accounts, or even certain bank accounts, those assets pass directly to your chosen person. Just be careful because if a name is outdated or incorrect, like an ex-spouse, it will still stand, even over what your will says.

A revocable living trust is often the best solution. It allows you to avoid probate entirely, keeps your affairs private, protects you while you're alive, and helps your heirs avoid unnecessary delays and costs. In my own case, we've set up a trust for our children that's structured to teach them financial responsibility over time. Their inheritance is managed by a trustee until they turn 25. From 25 to 30, they serve as co-trustees, while learning how to make decisions with guidance. At 30, they take full control. But even then, the trust still offers protection against things like divorce or lawsuits. We see it as a form of long-term parenting.

The truth is, estate planning isn't just about documents or legal strategy; it's about love. It's about protecting your family in the moments when they'll need it most. If you don't create a plan, the state will step in and create one for you. But it won't be designed with your values, your people, or your legacy in mind.

The right documents don't just protect your wealth. They protect your wishes. And more importantly, they protect the people you love.

PROTECT YOUR ASSETS FROM INVESTMENT FRAUD

Earlier in this book, you read about Bernie Madoff, who was the man behind the largest Ponzi scheme in history, who stole billions from highly educated, seemingly savvy investors. Unfortunately, financial predators don't always look like criminals. Sometimes, they're trusted family friends in nice suits who speak with authority and shake your hand with confidence.

Let me tell you a story I'll never forget.

The Oyster, the Lawyer, and the $2 Million Loss

Back in 2001, one of my long-time clients, a successful pharmacist, died suddenly after eating raw oysters at a local restaurant in June. (There's a reason for that old saying: *Don't eat oysters in months without an "R" in them.* It has to do with bacteria that thrive in warmer waters.)

This man wasn't just a great client; he owned three retail pharmacies and had a $2 million life insurance policy in place to care for his family. After the funeral, I called his widow. I didn't know her well, but I wanted to help. I told her the check was on the way and encouraged her to put the money in the bank, take her time, and not rush into any decisions about investing or paying off debts.

But she had other plans. She told me to send the life insurance proceeds directly to their attorney, who was a longtime family friend.

I hesitated, but eventually followed her wishes.

What followed was one of the most devastating financial frauds I've ever witnessed.

Over the next few years, that attorney, whom she had trusted with millions, gambled away the money. Not just her life insurance proceeds but also the money from the sale of all three pharmacies, proceeds from a wrongful death lawsuit against the restaurant, inherited funds, and money from other clients, including a man who sold his farm and lost everything he had saved for retirement.

Eventually, the truth came out. The attorney had been stealing from clients to fund a lavish lifestyle and gambling addiction. When the authorities closed in, he fled the country. The FBI later tracked him down in Madagascar, but the money was gone. Every penny.

His victims, including my client's widow, were left with nothing.

How to Protect Yourself from Investment Fraud

This story isn't meant to scare you; it's meant to wake you up. Because the people most at risk for financial fraud are the ones who think they're safe. They trust too much, ask too few questions, and assume that good manners mean good character.

Here's how to avoid that mistake:

1. Never trust just one person.

Split your financial relationships. Don't let one person control everything.

Consider working with three separate professionals:

- A CPA (Certified Public Accountant)
- A CFP® (Certified Financial Planner)
- An attorney

These professionals should be independent of each other. They shouldn't all work at the same firm, or worse, be close friends.

2. Don't rush big decisions.

Sudden wealth, whether from life insurance, inheritance, or selling a business, makes you a target. Take a breath. Park the money in a high-yield savings account. Think before you act.

3. Be alert to emotional manipulation.

Con artists are often charismatic. They know how to gain trust and make you feel safe. But remember this: being likeable doesn't make someone trustworthy.

4. "Trust, but verify."

That Russian proverb, made famous by President Reagan during the Cold War, applies perfectly here.[18] Even with people you trust, ask questions, demand documentation, and be involved.

---

18. Nina Porzucki, "Suzanne Massie Taught President Ronald Reagan This Important Russian Phrase: 'Trust, but Verify,'" *The World* (PRX), March 7, 2014, accessed September 9, 2025, https://theworld.org/stories /2014/03/07/suzanne-massie-taught-president-ronald-reagan-russian-phrase-trust-verify.

Protect Your Assets: Your Disaster Checklist

After watching eight seasons of *The Walking Dead*, I'd like to think I'd survive the zombie apocalypse. But after a quick self-assessment of my cardio, age, and general axe-handling skills, I've decided to prepare for more realistic disasters—ones we actually might face.

From raging wildfires to record-breaking hurricanes and global pandemics, we're living in an era where the unexpected has become . . . expected. In a world of nearly 8 billion people and unprecedented global connection, disruption is the new normal.

So here's the question: If a disaster hit your home tonight, would you be ready? Would your spouse or kids know where to find key documents? Life insurance policies? Account logins? Titles and deeds?

This checklist isn't for the end of the world—it's for the real world. Because being prepared is one of the best ways to protect your family, your finances, and your peace of mind.

Disaster Prep Checklist

Personal Records

Make copies and store securely (digitally and physically):

- ○ Driver's licenses
- ○ Passports
- ○ Social Security cards *(never carry in your wallet)*
- ○ Birth certificates
- ○ Marriage and divorce papers
- ○ Home deeds or titles
- ○ Car, boat, and RV registrations
- ○ Home inventory (room-by-room photos or video)

> **BAKER'S REMINDER:** Revisit the story of Ken Williams earlier in this book. He lost everything in a house fire and learned, the hard way, the value of a documented inventory.

Financial and Legal Records

Back up all digital files to a secure cloud platform. Also store paper copies in a fireproof/waterproof safe or bank safe deposit box.

Keep copies of:

- ○ All insurance policies (life, health, auto, homeowners, etc.)
- ○ Investment and retirement account records
- ○ Tax returns
- ○ Wills, living wills, and trusts
- ○ Financial and medical powers of attorney
- ○ Passwords and account access info (or at least a record of where to find them)

Use a good password keeper app—NOT in the Notes app on your Smartphone.

Here are some password apps you can check out: 1Password, Keeper, RoboForm, Bitwarden, Dashlane.

Stash Some Cash

During natural disasters, ATMs often go offline and gas stations hang signs reading "CASH ONLY." You don't want to be stuck with only a debit card during an evacuation.

Keep some emergency cash at home, stored securely. Enough to cover food, gas, lodging, and emergency needs for a few days. Trust me—it's a small move that makes a big difference.

WHAT HAPPENS WHEN, NOT *IF*

Let's be honest. One day, each of us will go. And when that time comes, will your family know where to find everything they need?

When my dad passed away, I had to play forensic accountant to help my mom collect his life insurance benefits. He had multiple policies where some companies had been acquired or merged over the years. No one was going to call us and offer that money. We had to hunt it down.

My Own Setup

In our fireproof safe at home, there's a three-ring binder labeled: "When I Die." Inside are:

- Copies of wills
- Insurance policies
- Investment statements
- Titles to all vehicles
- Key contact info
- My estate attorney's contact information

I even started drafting my obituary. I'm missing only one detail: the date I died. (I'm good—but not *that* good.)

FINAL WORD

Disaster planning isn't about paranoia; rather, it's about peace of mind. You won't regret taking the time to prepare . . . but you'll absolutely regret it if you didn't and something goes wrong.

It's about protecting your family from added stress, confusion, and hardship when they'll already be dealing with enough.

PRINCIPLE #12

Never Stop Your Financial Learning

The story of Curtis Carroll, better known as "Wall Street," is one of hardship, transformation, and unexpected triumph. Born into poverty in Oakland, California, Carroll grew up under the influence of drug dealers who taught him an early and brutal lesson: money equals power. But how to actually *get* that money was a mystery to him, and one that would be solved in one of the most unlikely places: San Quentin State Prison.

In 1996, at just 17 years old and unable to read, Carroll was sentenced to 54 years to life for murder during an armed robbery. The odds were stacked against him. Yet, in the confines of his prison cell, he began a journey that would redefine his life. Teaching himself to read through sheer determination, he soon gravitated to the financial section of the newspaper, captivated by the numbers and patterns of the stock market. This obsession earned him the nickname "Wall Street" and launched a personal mission to conquer the financial ignorance that had shaped his life.

Carroll didn't stop with himself. Recognizing that financial illiteracy was a systemic issue, especially among the poor and incarcerated, he began teaching others what he had learned. In his powerful TED Talk, he states: *"Financial illiteracy is a disease that has crippled minorities and the lower class in our society for generations—and we should be furious about that."* He challenges us to ask: *"How can 50% of Americans be financially illiterate in a country built on financial prosperity?"*[1]

---

1. Curtis Carroll, *How I Learned to Read—and Trade Stocks—in Prison*, TEDxSanQuentin, January 2016, video, 15:47, https://www.ted.com/talks/curtis_wall_street_carroll_how_i_learned_to_read_and_trade_stocks _in_prison.

He proves that the path to financial freedom, while not always easy, is not a mystery either. Financial literacy can be a powerful equalizer, granting freedom—real freedom—to those too often overlooked, marginalized, or written off by society.

Curtis Carroll's transformation reminds us that financial knowledge isn't reserved for the privileged or formally educated. It's something we all must pursue, often outside the walls of a classroom. Whether you're learning from the stock tickers in a prison newspaper or from the harsh realities of living paycheck to paycheck, financial education is a lifelong journey.

The truth is, most of us don't grow up learning how money really works. We're handed vague advice, piecemeal lessons, or worse, nothing at all. We stumble into adulthood with credit card offers in one hand and student loans in the other, expected to navigate a complex financial world with little more than trial and error.

But it doesn't have to be that way. Just like Curtis discovered in the most unlikely of places, the tools for financial empowerment are out there and the earlier you begin learning, the more powerful they become. Financial literacy is not a finish line; it's a habit, a mindset, and a set of principles that evolve with every stage of life.

FINANCIAL PODCASTS

Podcasts have become very popular for the younger generations. Explore the multitude of financial podcasts available and check out these below.

- **Money For the Rest of Us,** by J. David Stern, moneyfortherestofus.com
- **Planet Money**, by NPR Planet Money
- **HerMoney,** by Jean Chatzky Podcasts Archives
- **Mo' Money for Millennial Women**, by Jessica Moorhouse
- **Mo' Money Podcast | Personal Finance** with Jessica Moorhouse
- **BiggerPockets Money** by Mindy Jensen and Scott Trench, www.biggerpockets.com/podcasts/money
- **AffordAnything** by Paula Pant, affordanything.com/podcast

FINANCIAL BOOKS WORTH YOUR TIME

If you're the type who prefers to learn through books—whether in print, digital, or on Audible—there's no shortage of engaging and educational reads out there. The key is to find something that speaks to you and keeps you turning the pages.

One recent read that stood out to me was *The Big Short* by Michael Lewis,[2] which dives deep into the 2008 housing crisis. While it's not a personal finance how-to, it's a fascinating look at how systems fail and how a few people who understood the rules of money saw it coming. Financial literacy isn't just about budgeting and saving but also about understanding the world around you, and books like this expand that perspective.

Below is a list of titles ranging from practical guides to timeless wisdom that can help you continue growing your financial knowledge, no matter where you're starting from:

- **Get a Financial Life** by Beth Kobliner: A great beginner's guide for young adults looking to understand credit, savings, insurance, and more.
- **Broke Millennial** by Erin Lowry: Straightforward and funny, this book tackles everything from student loans to money conversations in relationships.
- **Women with Money** by Jean Chatzky: A practical and empowering guide for women looking to take control of their financial futures.
- **The Millionaire Next Door** by Dr. Thomas J. Stanley and William D. Danko: A classic that explores the habits and behaviors of everyday millionaires—and what sets them apart.
- **The Next Millionaire Next Door** by Thomas J. Stanley, PhD, and Sarah Stanley Fallaw, PhD: An updated continuation of the original, bringing fresh research and modern insights to timeless wealth-building strategies.

---

2. Michael Lewis, *The Big Short: Inside the Doomsday Machine* (New York: W. W. Norton & Company, 2010).

- **The Automatic Millionaire** by David Bach: Easy to read and inspiring, this book offers a straightforward plan to build wealth automatically. I used it for years in my class—it's that good.
- **Rich Dad Poor Dad** by Robert Kiyosaki: A foundational read in the world of personal finance. Kiyosaki's contrast between two financial mindsets makes it a compelling entry point for many.
- **Cheat Code: How to Win with Money Before Adulting Hits Hard** by Lindsey Baker, MAT, and Joe Baker, MBA: This is a companion piece to Baker's Dirty Dozen that is aimed at high school students.
- **Your Money or Your Life** by Vicki Robin and Joe Dominguez: For more than 25 years, *Your Money or Your Life* has been considered the go-to book for taking back your life by changing your relationship with money.
- **I Will Teach You to Be Rich,** by Ramit Sethi: It is a cross between a personal finance classic and a snarky Millennial manifesto.
- **The Book of Proverbs—The Bible**: This contains wise sayings that give advice about life, including money.

EXCELLENT FINANCIAL CALCULATOR WEBSITES

Smart money decisions start with solid numbers. These online calculators help take the guesswork out of financial planning:

- **Financial Calculators**: financialcalculators.com
- **Bankrate Calculators**: bankrate.com/calculators
- **Nerdwallet Financial Calculators**: nerdwallet.com/h/calculators/financial-calculators
- **Dinkytown Financial Calculators**: dinkytown.net
- **Bankrate 401(k) retirement savings calculator**: bankrate.com/retirement/401-k-calculator/
- **CalcXML Financial Calculators**: calcxml.com

TAP INTO FREE RESOURCES

We live in a time when financial education is more accessible than ever, and much of it is completely free. Whether you're looking for quick tips, deep dives, or just a fresh perspective, the internet is packed with quality content that can help you take control of your financial life.

YouTube has become one of the most powerful platforms for financial learning. Creators like Graham Stephan (with over a million subscribers) share real-world insights on everything from saving and investing to avoiding common money traps. His videos cover a wide range from, "How to Save 99% of Your Income" to house-flipping projects, making financial topics approachable and engaging.[3]

Here are a few additional trusted online resources worth exploring:

- **The Balance**: *"Make Money Personal"*
  A user-friendly site offering expert advice on budgeting, investing, managing debt, and even navigating career changes. (thebalancemoney.com)
- **Investopedia**: *"Sharper Insight, Better Investing"*
  One of the most comprehensive financial education sites available. Whether you're looking up terms, researching investment strategies, or exploring retirement planning, Investopedia has it all. (investopedia.com)
- **Kiplinger**: *"Personal Finance News, Investing Advice, Business Forecasts"*
  A long-standing leader in financial journalism. Great for staying updated on trends, tax tips, market outlooks, and long-term planning strategies. (kiplinger.com)
- **Bigger Pockets**: *"Create & Build Wealth With Real Estate Investing"*
  Learn more about investing in real estate. They provide a lot of resources for passive income. (biggerpockets.com)
- **Afford Anything**: *"You can afford anything . . . but not everything."*
  Blog with interesting forays into topics like investing, travel, lifestyle design, financial independence, and any other topic that jumps into this curiosity playground. Swap stories and ideas about

---

3. Check out his YouTube channel at https://www.youtube.com/grahamstephan.

real estate, entrepreneurship, productivity, personal development and a philosophy of money. (affordanything.com)

ONLINE PERSONAL FINANCE COURSES

- **Khan Academy**: *Personal Finance Courses*
Khan Academy, a nonprofit known for its free educational resources, offers a wide range of personal finance video lessons. Topics include everything from taxes and car expenses to paying for college. Curious whether it's better to lease or buy a car? Want to better understand budgeting or saving? These self-paced videos offer clear, practical guidance.[4]
- **Purdue University**: *Planning for a Secure Retirement*
This free online course includes 10 modules designed to help you plan for a successful retirement. Topics range from understanding your risk tolerance to simplified employee pensions. It's self-guided and ideal for those preparing for long-term financial security.[5]
- **University of Illinois Urbana-Champaign**: *Financial Planning for Young Adults (Coursera)*
Offered through Coursera, this introductory personal finance course is perfect for beginners. It covers goal-setting, budgeting, saving, investing, borrowing, and credit. The course takes about nineteen hours to complete and provides a strong foundation for young adults building their financial futures.[6]

As you continue your financial journey, I encourage you to keep exploring. The learning never stops and with so many resources available, there's no excuse not to keep growing.

---

4. https://www.khanacademy.org/college-careers-more/personal-finance
5. https://extension.purdue.edu/hhs/
6. https://www.coursera.org/learn/financial-planning

"Financial freedom is a mental, emotional,
and educational process."

Robert Kiyosaki

PRINCIPLE #13

True Wealth:
Serving Your Family, Community, and Faith

Alfred Bernhard Nobel (1833–1896) was a Swedish chemist, engineer, businessman, and prolific inventor. Best known for inventing dynamite, Nobel also owned Bofors, a major arms manufacturer, and at his career's peak, he controlled nearly a hundred factories producing explosives and munitions.

But in 1888, everything changed.

When Nobel's brother Ludvig died in France, a French newspaper mistakenly published an obituary for Alfred instead. The headline condemned him as "The merchant of death"—a man who had gotten rich by inventing ways to kill more people, faster. The article devastated Nobel. It offered a rare and brutal glimpse into how the world might remember him: not as a scientist, but as a dealer of destruction.

Determined to reshape that narrative, Nobel took action. He rewrote his will, dedicating the vast majority of his fortune, an estimated $265 million in today's dollars, to honoring those who "conferred the greatest benefit to mankind." His bequest established the Nobel Prizes, originally awarded in physics, chemistry, medicine, literature, and peace. (A sixth, for economics, was added in 1968.)[1]

In essence, Nobel was given a once-in-a-lifetime opportunity: to read his own obituary and rewrite the ending. Today, his name is no longer linked to explosives but to excellence, discovery, and peace.

---

1. Evan Andrews, "Did a Premature Obituary Inspire the Nobel Prize?" *History*, December 9, 2016, https://www
.history.com/articles/did-a-premature-obituary-inspire-the-nobel-prize.

As we return full circle to Baker's Dirty Dozen Principle #1: Find a Path That Will Fulfill You, I challenge you to reflect as Nobel did. Imagine reading your own obituary. What would it say? More importantly, what do you want it to say?

After 70 years on this earth, I've come to believe that financial steward-ship matters, but even more important is how you use your life, your talents, your time, and your energy to leave a meaningful mark on the world. That is the foundation of true wealth.

So yes, budget wisely, save diligently, and give generously. But above all, live with purpose. Use your gifts to make a difference. Spend your days loving well, forgiving freely, and walking with humility. That's the kind of wealth that endures.

APPENDIX

Essential Financial Principles for Success

BAKER'S CHEAT SHEET

- ◯ **Pursue a fulfilling path** – Ensure your personal, professional, and financial goals align with your values and aspirations.

- ◯ **Financial alignment with your partner** – Maintain open communication to ensure you and your significant other share financial priorities and goals.

- ◯ **Avoid lifestyle creep** – Live below your means to build long-term financial security.

- ◯ **Maximize employer-sponsored retirement plans** – Participate in options like a 401(k) and contribute as much as possible. At a minimum, contribute enough to receive the full employer match—it's free money.

- ◯ **Understand key investment categories** – The three major asset classes are (1) stocks, (2) bonds, and (3) cash equivalents.

- ◯ **Prioritize stock investments when young** – Younger investors should allocate more toward stocks for long-term growth.

- ◯ **Consider diversified retirement fund options** – Strong choices include (1) stock index funds and (2) target date funds.

- ◯ **Exercise caution with individual stocks** – Direct stock investments carry higher risk. Consider them only after maxing out retirement accounts and eliminating all debts except your mortgage.

○ **Prioritize debt repayment** – While not glamorous, paying off debt is crucial for financial well-being. For example, eliminating student loan debt with a 7% interest rate equates to a guaranteed 7% return.

○ **Establish a Roth IRA** – A stock index fund or target date fund are excellent options for funding your Roth IRA.

○ **Be mindful of debt** – While some debt may be necessary, there is no such thing as "good debt." Always pay credit card balances in full each month to avoid interest charges.

○ **Reevaluate luxury purchases** – An expensive vehicle is often an illusion of wealth rather than a sound financial decision.

○ **Track your spending** – Monitor both large and small purchases to maintain financial control.

○ **Negotiate prices** – Never accept the sticker price without attempting to negotiate.

○ **Be cautious with home purchases** – Avoid stretching your finances for a larger, more expensive house.

○ **Compare mortgage rates** – Even a 0.5% difference in interest rates can have a significant financial impact.

○ **Consider a 15-year mortgage** – If you opt for a 30-year mortgage, make additional principal payments to reduce long-term interest costs.

○ **Obtain proper insurance coverage:**
  • Renters insurance for liability protection
  • Homeowners insurance with a minimum of $500,000 liability coverage and replacement cost value on the property (dwelling and contents)
  • Auto insurance with a minimum liability of $500,000
  • A personal umbrella insurance policy of at least $1,000,000
  • Long-term disability insurance to protect income
  • Life insurance if others depend on you financially (term)
  • Health insurance, with consideration for a Health Savings Account (HSA) if available
  • A professional liability policy of at least $1,000,000, if applicable to your field

○ **Protect against identity theft** – Take proactive steps to safeguard personal and financial information.

○ **Commit to lifelong financial education** – Continue expanding your financial knowledge to make informed decisions.

Make a difference—leave a great legacy!

ABOUT THE AUTHORS

JOE BAKER, MBA

Joe Baker is an instructor at the University of Arkansas for Medical Sciences (UAMS) College of Pharmacy, where he has been teaching personal finance for over 26 years. He holds a Bachelor of Business Administration from Southern Arkansas University and a Master of Business Administration from the University of Central Arkansas.

Joe retired in 2019 from Pharmacists Mutual Company, where he spent 28 years providing insurance and financial services to pharmacists across Arkansas.

As part of his commitment to giving back to the community, Joe has endowed two scholarships. The first supports students from his hometown of Emerson, Arkansas, who are enrolled at Southern Arkansas University. The second scholarship benefits students at the University of Arkansas for Medical Sciences College of Pharmacy who attended Southern Arkansas University.

Joe has been a guest speaker for academic and corporate groups nationwide, promoting financial literacy.

Joe and his wife Brenda reside in Little Rock, Arkansas.

Joe Baker, MBA | Email: moneyworks365@gmail.com
Website: themoneycheatcode.com

Connect and follow
LinkedIn: www.linkedin.com/in/JoeBaker-MBA
Baker's Dirty Dozen on Facebook

LINDSEY BAKER, MAT

Lindsey Baker is a licensed teacher and writer with a passion for helping the next generation build strong foundations in life and money. With over a decade of experience in education, she has taught students in Arkansas, California, Palestine, Turkey, and Germany. Lindsey focuses on making complex topics accessible, engaging, and empowering for young learners.

Lindsey Baker, MAT | Email: themoneycheatcode@gmail.com
TikTok: @themoneycheatcode
Instagram: @themoneycheatcode
Website: themoneycheatcode.com

We would appreciate your feedback on what chapters helped you
most and what you would like to see in future books.

If you enjoyed this book and found it helpful,
please leave a review on Amazon.

Visit us at

THEMONEYCHEATCODE.COM

where you can sign up for email updates.

THANK YOU!